Emotional Self-Care for Black Women:

Boost Your Confidence & Mental Health with a Powerful Program in 90 Days!

Learn to Love Yourself, Increase Motivation, Overcome Obstacles & Become a Strong Woman.

By reading this document, the reader agrees that under no circumstances is the author responsible for any losses, direct or indirect, which are incurred as a result of the use of the information contained within this document, including, but not limited to, — errors, omissions, or inaccuracies.

About The Book

Have you ever wondered why many black women do not live to the fullest? In Emotional Self-Care for Black Women, you'll find out why. Many black women face different hurdles in their everyday lives, from anxiety to depression, low self-confidence, poor self-love, weakness, and many others. Many black women do not reach their potential because of the significant obstacles.

I understand that obstacles are a part of human existence. Yes, at some point in our lives, we would face struggles of some kind. But it is dangerous when these struggles become a constant in our lives. Not only will they begin to stunt our growth, but they will also begin to steal our joy until it remains of it. But the good news is this; we have tremendous power to control and dictate what happens to us or not. A lot of us do not know how powerful we are. We are much more powerful than we know. Until we rise into the actual knowledge of our greatness and power, we will have to keep dealing with some obstacles.

I'm pretty sure that you do not want that for yourself. I do not want it for myself either. No one does. I know you're getting curious about where I'm driving at. Don't be! I have come with solutions for every black woman dealing with obstacles of various kinds. Be it poor self-love to anxiety, lacking self-confidence, and every other thing that you can imagine.

I recommend reading this book wholly and carefully to get the best results. Don't be in a rush to finish it up that you read with so much speed and end up not assimilating everything. Also, this book will contain a ninety-day plan that will help you manage your emotions better.

Even if you think you've reached the end of the rope and can no longer go on, I assure you that this book will help you rise again. The time has come for you to regain all that you lost. Are you ready for this ninety-day journey to becoming the best version of yourself? Add this book to your cart, and let's begin!

Disclaimer!

This book has no medical backings, and it provides no mental health guarantee. Also, this book claims no authority over medical knowledge. This book is written based on what flows in my heart and what I have experienced. Note this down!

Introduction

For us to feel good emotionally, we have to look after ourselves.
— Sam Owen.

Some of us are very caring and amazing until we care for ourselves. We do the most important things for people without ever remembering to do those same things for ourselves. Tell me, are you not deserving of love, kindness, care, and awesomeness? You very much are. You are more than worthy of all of these. Taking care of oneself is an art. You need to learn one great art to become the best version of yourself. I see caring for one's oneself as nurturing. In this case, you are the flower. It would be best to have all the care you can get to flourish abundantly.

Many black women have missed out on essential points because they did not know how to combine self-care into their lives and blend it perfectly. I understand this from the depth of my heart because I used to be like this too. I was a very kind person. The kind that people would regard as a saint. You know, I loved and cherished public acceptance so much that I didn't realize when I made myself into a foot mat that people could walk on. I was in search of validation outside myself. That search drove me crazy. It has a way of making you do things you usually wouldn't do and tolerate crazy things just because you want that validation so bad. It is one of the most terrible and traumatizing things anyone could ever experience. I do not want you to repeat my mistakes and cry the tears I have cried. Instead, please learn from them to know how to deal with the obstacles that I faced. This book is very personal; it contains so much about me. I had to pour so much of myself inside. This book won't read like some science book or something out of a university lecture room. I find that quite boring. Black women do not like boring because they come from adventurous places. I will make this book very fun and relatable by including many personal experiences.

I am incredibly interested in black women who lack motivation too. I am no magician, neither do I have the power to push them back into creativity. But, one thing is sure. I'll help them rise to their feet again and find themselves and what they lost by assisting them in navigating all the parts that lead to creative inspiration. Dear black woman, I need to let you know that not having the required motivation every day is not as disastrous as many people make it seem. So, don't feel pathetic a bit. I know that you'll rise and walk into your motivation again. I think people do better and greater when they create and keep their motivation by themselves. Letting your inspiration reside in other people is not good at all. People are like the weather. They are very fluid. What becomes of you and your cause if the person that bears it fails? You might crumble. You should be your source and maintain all the motivation that you need.

I put a lot of energy and love into drafting a ninety-day plan in this book for women who are yet to master emotional management. Most times, people tend to think managing one's emotions is about not showing weakness in the face of trouble or putting up a faux strength. Not at all, gorgeous black woman. Managing your emotions is much more than that. Proper emotional management will help you be at your best even in situations that threaten your peace of mind or ruffle you too much. To be at your best in this context doesn't translate to keeping calm when you need to open your mouth to speak. Instead, it is about filling yourself with the right emotions for various situations. Yes, there is a thing like' right emotions.' Your right emotions are the appropriate emotions you should display in multiple cases. The truth is, different situations call for different emotions. That is why I advise you to learn how to manage your emotions well to react to different conditions. I'll write other chapters and let this plan come towards the end of the book. I find it fascinating doing that. Remember that saying about keeping the best for the last. Aye, that one.

This book contains simple and fun English for your reading pleasure. The personal stories in every part of the book will make it even more fun for you to read. Don't you think so? I also took women who do not always have time to read as they would desire into consideration while writing this book. How did I do it? Every section of this book contains 'Key Points,' which summarizes the chapter. So, you can read these key points and get great value from them. Now, isn't that wonderful? I believe this introduction has warmed you up and prepared you for all the wonder that you and I will explore in this book. The time has come for us to begin. So, open the

next page and behold the wonder of the first
chapter. I'll be with you through every word and
page. Read on, gorgeous soul!

Chapter One

How To Deal With Negative Emotions

Many black women do not know how to deal with negative emotions. I have seen lots of them blame themselves for feeling negative emotions. I used to blame myself and feel ashamed for having negative emotions too. I always felt that everyone had their lives in order except me. Not that I had a bad life, no. I had a good life. The good life I had always envisaged as a bit of child. But I tried to feel better by lying to myself that my life wasn't perfect enough because the negative emotions came. Maybe I would stop feeling depressed if I got the newest model of my favorite car brand. Maybe my anxiety would go away if that one person that always made me feel the butterflies would at least notice me. I got these things, yet the negative emotions wouldn't just stop. They worsened. All the things I desired came to me quickly to prove that they were not responsible for my negative emotions. Knowing that the negativity was from the inside made me feel worse. I felt ungrateful and wicked for not being happy with all I had.

My ignorance of negative emotions and how they affected people stayed with me for a very long time, and I wallowed greatly in it. I walked into the light that knowledge alone can give when I finally had the heart to see a therapist about the issue. I restricted myself from getting therapy because I considered it abnormal and crazy.

How could a person have a great life and still feel terrible inside? The first time I opened up to my therapist about the problem, he held my hand and smiled. He told me he knew what I was talking about, that he had experienced it too. I was shocked. It was so surprising to see that I wasn't the only one with the problem. It was even more pleasing that the therapist knew exactly how I felt. Even after a couple of sessions with the therapist, the negative emotions didn't disappear. Sometimes, I would listen to the therapist with great interest; other times, I could barely hear. But the therapist was a very patient man. Carefully and lovingly, he broke down all the walls I had built around myself. It took time. In all those therapy sessions, I learned so many things. My friend, emotions are not just emotions. They have a way of affecting our lives so much. Positive emotions have their way of lighting us up. Negative emotions also have their way of dimming our light. To reach your apex, you need to learn how to manage your emotions well and utilize them to your most significant advantage.

There is a truth that you must know about this emotion management thing. There is no perfect way to deal with emotions. One thing could work perfectly for you, and it might not work for someone else. I'll share methods and techniques that worked for me and how I employed them all. For someone like me who has encountered different kinds of people, I am well versed in emotions and how to manage them. So, you can trust me to be honest, practical, and kind with you as we journey through every page of this book.

Acceptance: a Vital Tool in Dealing with Negative Emotions

When people ask me the best way to deal with negative emotions, do you know the first thing I say? It is acceptance. You have to accept first that there is a problem before you can solve the problem. It might sound very simple and straight to the point, but it is not. Acceptance isn't all that easy and sweet.

Many of us deal with negative emotions today simply because we get to deal with the feelings without accepting them first. I am not asking you to revel in the negativity that negative emotions bring by acceptance. Instead, I am asking you to walk into the truth unafraid. What is the truth? That you are dealing with negative emotions and need help with them. I noticed that I healed faster from what I accepted than what I denied. I can tell you firmly that acceptance is the first and most crucial step you need to take if you succeed in dealing with all of your negative emotions.

It takes a lot of mental and emotional strength to accept negative emotions truly. Sometimes, you would try to make yourself feel good by choosing to live in denial of your reality. But no matter how much you do this, the emotions would still be there, lurking at your insides and waiting patiently to manifest. Untamed emotions have the power to ruin almost anyone. Do not ever make the mistake of giving your feelings a lot of energy. Most of our positive or negative feelings are not as powerful as we think they are. Yes, your emotions are not all that powerful. We are the ones that give power to our feelings. You know, the negative emotion eventually grows so much to become a monster capable of consuming you and making you sink into a lot of gloom.

I used to listen to sorrowful songs to elicit some catharsis in the past. Listening to sorrowful songs would make me cry, and crying always made me feel better after an episode of sadness. I thought it was an excellent coping mechanism. I only realized how bad it was when I became obsessed with sad music. I'd think up my sadness and weep. It became that terrible. Do not ever make the mistake of making negativity a part of your coping mechanism. It always doesn't end well.

***

You have to master the act of acceptance. It is a skill that you must possess if you genuinely desire to deal with your negative emotions. No matter how ugly, terrible, and heartbreaking those emotions you feel are, denying them won't do you any good. Denying them empowers them. It is perfectly normal to feel negative emotions. A lot of us do. But, we devise various methods to deal with them. The happiest people sometimes go through their bouts of negative emotions. Negative emotions do not come because you are a terrible person. Negative emotions happen because you are human, and humans are emotional beings who can feel a vast range of emotions. There's no need to beat yourself up about how you feel. You're not some work of AI which is programmed to feel a certain way all the time. You are a beautiful black woman with emotions.

Look deep into yourself, embrace and accept the truth of every negative emotion that you feel. Think of those emotions as minor problems that you can handle. You have all that you need to deal with them, trust me. You have to quit wallowing in your negative emotions. You have to wake up each morning and choose a positive emotion like joy. But this can't happen without acceptance. My gorgeous black woman, you are lovely even with the negativity you feel. Your emotions are only a sign that you are human. Accept them today. Acceptance will always make you do better and manage them better. Please do not be ashamed to accept them. It's one of the best things you could ever do to take charge of your negative emotions.

Key Points

I am writing this key points section to make everything easy and fun. This section contains the key points that I need you to remember always as you journey towards accepting your negative emotions.

1. Acceptance is a vital tool that you must embrace to successfully deal with your negative emotions.

2. Please don't beat yourself up for feeling the way you do, we are humans, and emotions make up a large chunk of our humanity.

3. Acceptance is the first step you need to take when dealing with negative emotions.

4. You have everything you need to fight your negative emotions and win. You are way stronger than you think you are.

5. Your emotions are strong, yes. But it is the emotion you give a lot of attention to that will thrive the most in your life.

Allow Yourself to Feel

Many of us feel trapped in our negative emotions because we do not allow ourselves to feel them the way we should. We are very quick at stopping our emotions just before anything happens. A lot of black women mistake this behavior for strength. You know, strong women do not shed tears when they should. Strong women do not spend a lot of time being emotional. Strong women do not allow help in their lives, and they rather sweat it out. Who made these rules? Again I ask, who made these rules? You have to unlearn these things. Being a strong woman doesn't translate to being a woman who hides her humanity and sensitivity. Being a strong woman doesn't stop you from exploring your emotions. But, do not allow your emotions to take absolute control of your life. I am afraid of identifying with the word 'strong' sometimes. I wouldn't say I like all the misconceptions that surround it. Many people think to be strong is to throw away all the softness that makes you human. No, that is not what it means to be strong. Do not call me strong if that's what it means to you.

I love to embrace my humanity and bask in the fullness of it. It is what makes me who I am. It is also what makes you who you are. You know, right? Never for any reason throw your humanity away. Doing that will make you into a woman that you will not love. I have often tried to harden my heart because of some bad encounters that I had in the past. Whenever I noticed the slightest shift in energy and behavior towards me, I'd quickly move away in a bid to protect myself from emotional troubles. Doing it saved me from many emotional problems and disappointments, but I regret it now. It stopped me from making meaningful relationships and being as human as I could be. I tried so hard to stop inhibiting myself from feeling, but I could not. I had gotten so deep into it that I had to invest so much energy in letting myself feel things the way I wanted to. Now, I don't do that anymore. I give no one the power to make me into a person I am not.

Now, you'd wonder. Do we allow ourselves to feel just the good things? Is it okay to let one's self feel negative emotions, too? The answer is yes. Let yourself feel both positive and negative emotions. Nothing expresses your humanity and human weakness more than the expression of emotions. Allow yourself to be as joyful as you want. Also, allow yourself to cry and feel the pain the way you want to. No, this is not bad advice. I promise. Feeling good emotions fills one with joy and strength.

Regarding the negative ones makes one heal faster. It is high time that people stop thinking negative emotions are synonymous with weakness. I have learned that shutting away negative feelings doesn't help at all. Shutting them away causes them to hide in the deepest parts of you. They'd lie in wait for triggers and descend on you on the days you least expect.

Shutting away negative emotions is like treating the symptoms of an illness without dealing with the root cause, which is the primary illness. At some point, the symptoms will disappear. You'll be under the illusion that the disease disappeared too. But it never goes away. It'll shelter itself in one part of your body and come out later. It always comes out worse. It is for this reason that you must deal with the root cause. Deal with the depression, fear, anxiety, and other negative emotions you feel. Allow yourself to handle them. Cry, wring your hands in despair if you want, scream out some sadness, feel it all you want. After feeling them all, what comes next? I know this is the question standing at the tip of your tongue now. I'll answer.

After feeling them, brace up and deal with them. It is one thing to let yourself feel emotions, and it is another thing to dwell for a very long time in them. Embracing your feeling has its unique way of making you heal very fast. After feeling it, pick yourself up and work towards putting an end to the negative emotions. My dear, you must understand that this whole thing is a gradual process. It doesn't happen all at once. But the more consistent you are at it, the faster it becomes. Some women can heal all by themselves, but some can not. That doesn't make them weak. If your healing or rising requires you to undergo therapy, do not be afraid or ashamed to experience it. It is your life, and you matter the most. Your opinion of yourself is the greatest there is, do not let other people's opinions of you take up so much space in your life. Remember, it is your own life.

Key Points

1. It is okay to feel negative emotions. But it is not okay to dwell in them.

2. Do not shut away from your negative emotions. Let yourself feel.

3. Basking in the softness of your humanity doesn't make you weak. It is proof that you are human.

4. You have everything that you need to deal with your negative emotions. You are a lot stronger than you think you are.

5. Do not let bad encounters stop you from showing affection and interacting with people. Do not give anyone the power to make you into who you are not.

Choose Positivity

Almost everything in life involves decision-making. Most things that go on in our lives result from our choices. Choosing isn't limited to any area of our lives. You can choose positive emotions in place of negative ones. Don't get ruffled yet, and I understand it is no stroll in the park. I have learned that most things that involve choosing are not very easy to choose from, no matter how simple they may seem to be. Sometimes, I like to choose something that goes on in my life. Other times, I'm not too fond of it. Decision-making is one thing that I cannot afford to do wrongly. A small decision could make or mar my life.

Your decision-making power can also help you fight negative emotions. How? Most emotions are either positive or negative. You can choose to go with the positive ones and expel the negative ones out of your mind. Of course, it isn't easy at all. The first thing I would advise you to do as you begin to choose positive emotions is the identification of your triggers. In simple terms, triggers are the things that propel your feelings. For example, you begin to feel very terrible after seeing a test result at school. You feel awful because you performed poorly on that particular test. We can say the poor performance is the trigger. Choosing positive emotions doesn't end at making the decision. That's where it begins. You have to take deliberate steps to make it easy for your choices to manifest.

Look deep inside of you and try to pinpoint all that spur your negative emotions. Are they things within or beyond your control? If they are within your control, do yourself and your emotional health the good of controlling them. What happens when they are beyond your control? That is the point where it all becomes somewhat tricky. Here, you'd have to devise a plan that can keep the trigger away from you as long as possible. My dear woman, I understand the fear that comes with detachment. Even if that one thing that you're detaching yourself from had shrunk you into a lot of smallness in the past, you'd still experience that fear. Humans seem to fear detachment more than they do a lot of things. With detachment, a lot of things

change. But one thing is sure, detaching yourself
from the things that trigger your negative side is
a great thing to do no matter what.

After dealing with the triggers, you'll come to
realize that choosing positivity is not as complex
as you once thought. It is one thing to choose
positive emotions. It is another thing to be
consistent at picking them. Choosing positivity is
not a one-time thing at all. It is something that
you would need to do frequently. You don't
select positive emotions today and dwell in
negativity tomorrow. No, it doesn't work like
that. With the dawn of every new day, you
choose positivity all over again. You don't have
to make it a routine. I find patterns as boring as
hell. You could make it an enjoyable and easy
process for you. I love to choose positive
emotions through affirmations. I could decide to
affirm ten wholesome things that involve
positive feelings when I wake up. Something like
this;

I embrace positive emotions today. I am not
overwhelmed by any form of negativity today.
It looks fun, right? It is a lot of fun, and it is
stress-free. It works great too. I think you'd love
it so much. Just try it first and see the wonder it
bears.

Key Points

Choosing positive emotions is no easy thing, but
I trust in your ability and strength to do it and do
it well. Below are the essential points for this
section. Keep them close to your heart always.

1. Amidst all the negative emotions you feel, you can choose positive emotions if you desire.

2. Choosing positive emotions is not an easy thing, but I believe you can do it.

3. Do not be afraid to detach yourself from anything that triggers negativity in you.

4. Be bold in choosing positive emotions.

5. You have all it takes to fight your negative emotions. Yes, you are powerful like that.

My dear black woman, this is where this chapter ends. Apply all I have shared with you in this chapter to your own life, and you'll notice a significant improvement. Now, come along with me to a new chapter. The next chapter will be centre on self-love. Self-love is one thing that many of us do not fully understand. Trust me to unveil it to you in all its glory in the next chapter!

Chapter Two

Self-Love and The Black Woman

Love yourself enough to set boundaries. Your time and energy are precious. You get to choose how you use it. You teach people how to treat you by deciding what you will and won't accept. —Anna Taylor.

I have come to learn that a lot of black women have very wrong definitions of self-love. Self-love is beyond posting gorgeous photographs of yourself on social media and using the caption #selflove. If it were this simple and plain, we would all love ourselves, and there would be no hate in the world, but self-love transcends this. True self-love is the most fantastic romance ever. Nobody can rob you of this kind of romance. It is deeper and more authentic than romantic relationships with other people who can let go at any time.

Now, what does self-love mean? Self-love is all about looking out for yourself in every area of your life. Self-love acquaints you with the truth that you are the first, most important, and most influential person in your life. No matter how much you love other people, do not forget that you come first. Sometimes, people forget this truth. They seem not to remember their importance in their own lives. Forgetting one's importance is one of the most dangerous things that can ever happen to anyone. In the past, I used to sacrifice a lot for people and do many uncomfortable things because I thought it was cool to express love to the people who mattered to me. Now, I am unlearning a lot of things. No, my heart did not evolve into stone. I am still full of love. But I am learning not to show love to people to my detriment.

Do you know that self-love is not selfish? Yes, you are not greedy for loving yourself the way you do. You are not a selfish person for choosing to love yourself with the whole of your heart. I'd love to recount a story my friend once shared with me. My friend had a classmate who everyone said was the kindest girl in school. Some said she was an angel. Do you know why this girl was called an angel? It was because she never said no to anyone. She was from a wealthy family who cared deeply about her and bent to her every whim. So, she always had the things she wanted. My friend admitted to envying her sometimes. Tell me, what fifteen-year-old wouldn't envy such a sweet life? Despite how gorgeous and rich that girl was, she had very low self-esteem and just a droplet of self-love in her. She greatly desired to be everyone's friend. She wanted to be loved by all. But that's an impossible thing. After trying to no avail, she resorted to giving gifts to her classmates. They would all jump at her and display faux affection towards her. They did that because they wanted the things they or from her to keep coming. Almost everyone in the class disliked how she threw herself in their faces. But who would dare confront the richest babe in class who gave everyone gifts like she was Father Christmas?

Her kindness continued for a while. Everything became sour when some greedy classmates coerce her to give away everything that she had nothing left for herself. She was able to do it for a while. When she got fed up with the whole thing, she stopped. No one knows what gave her the courage and wisdom to control. She faced a lot of hate, mockery, and subtle criticisms from the people she gifted the most important things. But, she never went back to her old self again until they all left school. Do you know what I told my friend when she shared this story with me? I told her that the girl began to love herself when she stopped being the sweet and cheerful giver. That was the point of realization for her. I still wonder what the propelling force was. I also wonder if she sat herself down and talked honestly to herself. Sometimes, you are the only one that can tell yourself the truth.

Just like the girl in this story, people may begin to despise you and call you selfish for deciding to stop sucking up to anyone and standing up for yourself, and loving yourself with all your heart. My dear black woman, pay them no mind. It is better to be labeled selfish for loving yourself instead of being called kind for giving your self-love up for anyone. I repeat this, do not let anyone rob you of the love you have for yourself. If loving yourself requires you to be 'selfish' and 'distant,' do it. It might hurt at first, but you'd love the outcome eventually. Sometimes, people try to make us feel terrible for loving ourselves the way we do and carrying ourselves with so much elegance. Never give room for that. Do not let it thrive at all.

Many black women stay back in places that do not help them because they do not know the true essence of self-love. Self-love makes you walk out of a room that reeks of disrespect. Self-love makes you ignore the people who try to make you into who you are not. In our quest to be loved by people, we need to realize that we need to love ourselves first. Your love for yourself is what matters the most. You'd still feel horrible if a thousand people loved you and you did not love yourself. The journey to self-love is not an easy one. It is not impossible either. Are you willing to go on that journey?

Begin first by forgiving yourself for all the times you did not love yourself right. I ask this of you because people tend to beat themselves up about things they did wrongly in the past when they find out the right things. Count your past experiences as lessons that shaped you. No matter what happens, I do not find myself regretting some of the not-so-great things I did in the past. I don't regret them because they were all a part of my becoming. I think you should embrace this ideology too. Not only does it keep you from breaking up, but it also helps you learn from your mistakes and past experiences.

Today, decide to love yourself fully no matter what happens.

Key Points

Self-love is no easy thing. But it becomes much easier when you know your worth. Also, you must realize that you come first in your own life. Knowing this will help you love yourself as you should. Below are the critical points for this section.

1. You come first in your life.

2. Your opinion about yourself is the essential thing in your life. Every other one is secondary.

3. Your love for yourself is the most honest there is.

4. Do not compromise your self-love to please one. No one is worth your self-love.

5. Do not allow anyone to make you feel terrible for loving yourself the way you do. You are worth it, and you'll forever be.

People Love and Treat You the Way You Do To Yourself

The way you love yourself is the way people will love you. The way you treat yourself is the way people will treat you. Someone once said these words to me. That first time, it all sounded crazy to me. I wondered if people would genuinely treat me terribly if I treated myself terribly. I thought of human kindness and dwelled in it. People will be kind to me even if I don't treat myself well, and people are kind. It took me quite a while to realize that I am not entitled to people's kindness. Hold on. I'll explain this to you. Some of us are naturally kind and loving. We expect other people to be kind and caring like us most of the time. We do not prepare ourselves for the truth. The truth is, the world contains a variety of people, people who don't share the same beliefs as us. We have to prepare our minds for these kinds of people, so we don't feel hurt when we encounter them. I am excited about extraordinary times and good people, but that doesn't stop me from mentally preparing myself for people whose beliefs and attitudes differ from mine. These people are everywhere. You could bump into them in the stores, and you could meet them on the bus too. Anywhere. Meeting them unprepared is one crazy thing that could happen to anyone.

Like I told you earlier, it took me time to realize the integrity of those words. But now, I keep it close to my heart. You should, too. People will most likely do the same if you show yourself so much, love. If you treat yourself like a Queen, you'll get the same regal treatment from people. Come to think of this. You have this gorgeous dress that makes people drool when you wear it.

One day, you decide to make the magnificent dress into a rag by using it to clean. You expect the people around you to discourage you from using it as a rag, right? Or, they'd help you wash it and keep it safe. The chances of these happening are very slim. Most people would join you in using the dress to clean. If the owner can use this dress while cleaning, who am I not to? Then they'd go on and use it too. Do you understand the message I'm trying to convey with this brief illustration? People love and treat you just the way you do to yourself. Whenever you begin to notice that people treat you terribly, pause and think about how you've been treating yourself before those people; in that, you'll find your answer. I know you want to be loved and treated like royalty. But it won't just start happening. You have to put in the work by doing it to yourself first. Understanding this will help you a great deal.

Don't allow anyone to fool you into believing that you are not worthy of love and good treatment. You are more than worthy of it. From time to time, you might meet people who would try to scorn you into self-loathing. These people are adept at making people feel like they do not matter. I beg of you, do not give such people the opportunity to thrive where you are. No matter how great some of them pretend to be, never entertain them. It would help if you always looked out for negative signs like insensitive jokes, hatred, and other similar factors that very flashy personalities may mask. It would interest you to know that some of these people come dressed as your friends. They'd get into you by befriending you. As time progresses, you'll see that they do not mean well for you.

I used to have a friend that did these things to me. He'd call me arrogant for carrying myself the way I did and doing things the way I did them.

He'd make me feel like I intimidated people with my presence by just being myself. Of course, I thought it was good advice at first. I thought I had a friend who cared about me so much. But my doubts began to grow when I found myself living a life I had once detested. I became highly reclusive because my friend said I was 'too much. I didn't realize how much I needed a brain reset until I slid into my solitude to have a heart-to-heart talk with myself. I'm the most honest person when it involves talking to myself. I thought about the strangeness I felt with myself and new behaviors. I realized I was a stranger to myself already, which had to change.

When I finished dwelling in my thoughts, I ended that friendship. It wasn't exactly easy because I had grown attached to that friend. But it was worth it in the end. Sticking with a friend who is against the great love you have for yourself is not worth it at all. Please don't make my mistakes. I shared my story with you because I was hoping you could learn from it. I hope you do. If you've been treating yourself poorly and not loving yourself as you should, the time has come for you to step up. Tell me, don't you want the royal treatment that comes with being good to yourself? Don't you want to inspire people to treat you great by first treating yourself great? I am confident that you do. It is no easy thing, primarily if you're used to not being good to yourself. But you can start now and still excel at it. Start with the little things. Respect yourself, carry yourself with pride, and love yourself. As time goes on, you'd grow into loving yourself in the most significant ways.

Suppose you genuinely want people to treat you exceptionally and love you as you desire. In that case, you have to begin it with yourself first. The way you love and treat yourself is an inspiration to treat you. Find the critical points for this section below.

1. People love and treat you the way you love and treat yourself.

2. Prepare yourself to meet humans with varieties of characters the moment you step outside your home.

3. When you notice that people maltreat you, take a pause and evaluate the way you've been treating yourself.

4. Love yourself wholly.

5. Do not accept poor treatment from people.

On Self-Love and Forgiveness

Forgiveness is one crucial thing that a lot of people ignore. Whenever the topic of forgiveness comes up, what comes to your mind? To forgive is to let go of resentment, pain, anger, or vengeance you feel towards a person or a thing. Forgiveness makes you decide not to take revenge for the wrong done to you. It makes you not pay back evil with evil. Since I started this forgiveness part of this book, has it ever occurred to you that you need some forgiveness? Not from anyone but yourself. I'll make this easier for you and me by simply talking about self-hate and bitterness. You might wonder if there are people who do hate themselves.

Yes, some people do hate themselves. But self-hate doesn't just happen. Something always triggers it. There are a lot of things that could cause self-hate. For some, it is body shaming. For others, it is low self-esteem and depression. Then some people hate themselves for making mistakes and going through terrible experiences. Many people have done things that they are not proud to say. I have made a couple of errors that taught me lessons. I need to remind you that self-hate and self-love do not exist in the same place. You cannot love yourself if you hate yourself as they are two perfect opposites. They can't dwell in one person simultaneously.

And this is where forgiveness comes in. Have you truly forgiven yourself for that mistake that you made? Are you willing to move on and become a better version of yourself? Come on, let us explore forgiveness together. Growing up, I heard this phrase a lot. 'Forgive and Forget.' But in my adult life now, I know that it is an impossible thing to do. We don't forget. We can only forgive. Healing is one of the most gradual processes ever. You could try the best healing methods in one day, but you won't heal in just one day. You need to slow down and walk into your healing gallantly. Of all forms of forgiveness, I think self-forgiveness is the most difficult one. You'll wake up and blame yourself almost every day. You'll weep and wish to go back in time to undo a lot of things.

Self-forgiveness is no magic. On some days, you'll experience faux healing and think you've finally forgiven yourself, only to fall into sorrow later. Despite how difficult and demanding forgiving is very much possible. Pour yourself into it.

You can start by acceptance. Living in denial is terrible. It steals your peace. I know acceptance hurts, but it is a hurt that you need to embrace if you genuinely desire to forgive yourself fully. Tell yourself that what happened. Yes, you made a mistake, and you regret it. Forgiveness begins with acceptance. When you finish with it, give yourself some time to feel pain. It would trigger some cathartic tears. Crying makes me feel better every time. It doesn't only clear the fog in my head. It also reduces the pain in my chest. Don't you find it interesting how internal hurt begins to manifest as physical pain? It intrigues me.

Cry all you want. Then stop. Afterward, do away with the things that trigger your self-hate. They could be objects, people, and places. I understand that you cannot avoid all of these things altogether, but ensure to avoid the ones you can. Being exposed to too many triggers can mess with your healing process. Don't expect to heal at once. Go easy and take your time. Don't let anyone make you feel terrible for healing and forgiving yourself the way you do. Believe in your healing and forgiveness. You'll forgive yourself and stop hating yourself, trust me. It might seem impossible at first, but you'll see how you'll do it like magic.

How do I know I have forgiven myself? There are no perfect ways to know, my dear. But you'll see when you encounter a trigger and not falter. When the desire for revenge no longer burns inside you. When you successfully forgive yourself, you'll appreciate the beauty of self-love more and let it flow into you. Allow yourself to be full of self-love. Let it engulf you. It is one of the most beautiful things ever. Forgive yourself, then love yourself with all that is in you.

Key Points

I hope you forgive yourself with all the forgiveness that you need. Love yourself with joy and pride. You're a wonder! Below are the key points you could note for this section?

1. Self-hate and self-love do not thrive together. You have to make a pick from these two.

2. Healing and self-forgiveness are two very gradual processes. Be kind to yourself.
3. No one on earth can love you the way you love yourself.

4. Acceptance is the very first step towards true forgiveness. Please don't skip it.

5. Exposing yourself to your triggers can mess up your healing process. Try your best to stay away from them as much as you can.

6. Don't permit anyone to make you feel bad for healing and forgiving yourself the way you do.

Again, we have come to the end of a chapter. I hope you love this chapter, and I hope it does help you understand self-love better. I put a lot of love into this chapter just for you. Go on and forgive yourself. Fill the space that once housed your self-hate with nothing but love. Now, come with me. Let us explore anxiety together. Anxiety is another major thing that troubles black women

Chapter Three

The Black Woman Fights with Anxiety

Our anxiety does not empty tomorrow of its sorrows but only empties today of its strengths. —C.H. Spurgeon.

Anxiety is one disorder that almost everyone experiences at some point in life. It usually comes with persistent worrying, and sometimes, fear about everyday situations. The worry that comes with anxiety isn't anything like the usual one that you and I know. This type comes with tremendous weaknesses and limitations. The kind of limitation that stops you from taking the one step you need to take to live your dream life. A lot of people do not understand anxiety. That's why they call it bluff when people with anxiety voice out the things that keep them from sleeping at night. My dear black woman, do not get sad over the actions of such people. Your feelings are valid. Do you know one thing that we should take seriously in today's world? Mental health education.

Anxiety is one disorder that can make a great mess of enormous efforts if ignored. It is a problem. But thankfully, it has a solution. Many black women are yet to find the help they need to deal with their anxiety because they do not accept anxiety. Many reasons cause this lack of acceptance—the most typical being that they consider it a terrible feeling. This great need for acceptance in the human race causes some people to lie to themselves and deny their glaring realities to be accepted by other people. I tell people, acceptance is a significant thing that you should embrace in the emotional self-care journey.

Remember the title of this book? It's all about emotional self-care. YOUR emotional self-care. I need you to know that acceptance is not something anyone can do for you but for yourself. You should also know that anxiety is no death sentence nor a contagious disease that you should hide. It is part of human life. Your anxiety level is way higher than other people's, which doesn't make you a terrible person. All you need is help to manage your anxiety. But, tell me, how can you get help for a disorder you claim not to have? It's impossible. Do you get my point now? In your acceptance of your anxiety, you will find the help you need.

Well, acceptance isn't the only thing there is to deal with anxiety. It is only the first. After acceptance, what happens next? Get help. Help means different things to different people. It is getting therapy and speaking to experts in anxiety disorder management. The truth is, no one can help you as much as a good therapist can in things like this. Sometimes, a good friend could give you the listening ears you need and a shoulder to lean your head. But your friend most likely won't be able to get you the help you truly need. Except your friend is a therapist, of course. I've met many people who overlook things they should pay attention to because they 'talked' to their friends. No, I'm not trying to make light of the help friends render. I'm simply trying to make you understand the importance of professional help in cases like this. Therapists undergo a lot of training to help you deal with anxiety, trust them to do all they can to help you. It isn't as easy as I make it seem, right? I know, Luv.

I used to be hesitant about therapy in the past too. I'd feel ashamed and wonder what the therapist would think of me later. I'd wonder if the therapist would see me as some pitiful human or someone who needed help. It took me a while to stop overthinking the whole thing. It was so overwhelming! There is no shame in getting help, and there is no shame in seeing a therapist. You do not only do yourself good, but you also help the people around you- your friends, family, colleagues, and other people you would have to meet in your life. When we suffer illnesses or face challenges, we are not always the only ones that suffer them. The people close to us and those who love us do, too. The bond we share with them always gets affected. You love your folks too much to watch them suffer for your sake, don't you? I know you do. Please don't make them suffer by giving your anxiety the power to eat deeply into you.

You could also fight anxiety by choosing to worry about a few things. Try to take your mind away from irrelevant things. Everything isn't worth your peace. It is perfectly okay to worry but don't let it get the better of you. You can minimize your worrying by creating a simple list of what you should pay mind. This method is one of the most effective methods to deal with anxiety.

Creating a simple list has a way of taking your concentration and worry from everything. It'll help you focus on the things on the list squarely. You would love it. I have always created to-do lists so long that I do not even remember the exact time I started building them.

Anxiety is not a one-day fight. You have to invest your time, energy, and resources into fighting it. Also, your victory in the battle depends majorly on you. Now, take a deep breath and ask yourself a question. Am I ready to win this fight? Yes! Your victory begins the very moment you decide to stand up and fight. You already have what it takes to win. At first, fighting anxiety may feel like a lost battle. But it is not. The emotional liberation and joy from winning are worth all the fight. Don't you think so, too?

Anxiety disorder affects the physical body as well. Ever been in a situation where you cannot breathe well because you're so anxious about what's going to happen next? I'll share a personal experience with you. I worked in a laundry store for almost a month. On a fateful day, something happened. We were about to lock up the store that day. I dealt with severe fatigue, and I couldn't wait to go home. I was about to leave when a man brought in some clothes for washing and handed them over to me. He said, "Alright, take these, just a top and a pair of jeans, get them all clean before uhm... Friday." That day was a Monday. I stood up from where I was and took the clothes from the man. I casually dropped them inside a small laundry basket and zoomed off. Coming in the next day, I couldn't find the clothes anymore.

The shop was relatively small, so I checked every part of it properly in about five minutes. I came out with nothing. Immediately, I had a nervous breakdown. My head began spinning, and my heartbeat had become exceedingly fast. I had been employed there for less than a month, and a customer's clothes had gone missing? Bullshit. Throughout the week, it became a routine. Anytime I approached the shop in the morning, my heart would start beating twice as fast. I'd ransack the store again, and when I found nothing, the situation worsened. And it would be the same for about nine hours till I left for home. For seven days, I had that thing going on.

The owner of the clothes soon came looking to grab his clothes, and as I stood fidgeting before him, I decided to ask him what he had given me. Ridiculous right? "You're asking me what laundry I gave to you. How am I sure you haven't given my clothes to another person? I need the clothes for an occasion tomorrow!"

To make matters worse, he was a first-timer. What an impression! I said to myself, "you're gonna get sacked after this." I somehow managed to hold my ground, and of course, he had to remind me. It took a lot of courage to do that, by the way, something we're going to look at later on this lovely ride. To cut an already long story short, I hope I didn't bore you, though. After he explained how the clothes he brought looked like, I discovered it was sitting right in front of me all the while and I was looking at it for days but never knew it was the one. Due to the fatigue, I felt when he brought the clothes. My mind painted a red shirt and a blue pair of jeans and what he got was an orange-colored shirt and a couple of black pants! You know, as much as I was so happy, I was disappointed as well. What if I had developed a heart attack and collapsed? All because of what I thought I lost but was still there? Haha, the mind finds ways to play tricks on us sometimes. But as we grow, we should get acquainted with those tricks and know-how to handle them when they come. It's a simple story, but I hope you understand the illustration I tried to paint. Anxiety will come, but do your best not to let it get the best of you.

Key Points

The fight against anxiety can turn out to be victorious if you do it right. Doing it right simply means being patient with yourself and giving your very best. I believe in your abilities, and I am confident that you will win. Below are the key points that you should note for this section.

1. The fight against anxiety is a gradual process. Please, be kind to yourself.
2. You have fought many things with ease, and anxiety would be no exception.
3. Getting professional help is a great way to combat anxiety.
4. Pay mind to the important things alone.
5. Your victory against anxiety disorder begins with acceptance.
6. Anxiety has physical side effects.

Worrying Comes With No Gain

Worrying comes with no gain. It only knows how to drain you and leave you weak and frustrated. I think a lot of people do believe that worrying can change things. Sorry to disappoint you, darling. It has no gains at all.

I'm not judging you for worrying or getting worked up the way you do. I understand you perfectly. I have interacted with many people, black women especially, in living this life. I made a beautiful discovery. Worry is the fate of intelligent and active minds. Several studies have attested to this truth too. It takes a busy mind to think about things that most people ignore. But, you have to control your worrying lest it robs you of things that you cherish.

Instead of worrying, you could try finding a solution to the things that make you worry. That is one of the most effective ways to handle worry. I remember staying up late into the night sometimes in high school, worrying about how I'd fare in my exams. My friend discovered my excessive worrying and asked, 'why not study instead?' That one question changed me considerably. Whenever I begin to worry about things, I ask myself, 'why not fix it instead? Why not find a solution?' I listened to my friend that night and studied instead. I got a good grade on my exam, and I am forever thankful for that friend.

Whenever the worries begin to trouble you, seek out a solution.

Sometimes, this method won't work—when you have no control over the things that make you worry. Worrying about the things we can't change does us no good. I understand how difficult it is to stop thinking about things that make us worried but cannot change. It feels like hell. You'd feel this helplessness deep inside of you, but there's nothing you can do about it.

Worrying about things we can't change is of no benefit to us. It is not a behavior that we should embrace for any reason. My dear woman, please strive to stop beating yourself up about things you have no control over. For a long time in my own life, I did this thing. I don't think mine can pass as a worry, though. Maybe it is. When I was younger, I had these very chubby hands that made my classmates laugh at me. Kids find humor in absurd things sometimes. Some of my classmates said my hands looked like fat chicken laps. Sometimes, I'd cry and cuss out anyone who said mean stuff about my hands. I'd think about how to 'fix' my hands for hours at school. I think my performance at school would have been better if I didn't spend a lot of time worrying about my hands. My eight-year-old brain did a lot of work worrying about my hands. My folks at home always said I had the cutest hands ever, but I chose to believe the kids. I think humans have a knack for believing the bad things people say to them and throwing all the good ones into the bin.

Do you know what made me stop worrying about my hands? I sat my ass down on a chair and talked to myself. I am always the most honest person when it comes to me. I grew up that way. That day, I spoke to myself and acknowledged the truth that there was nothing I could do to make my hands like other people's hands. You know, I'm too full of uniqueness to contain a thing that is not me. Somehow, I saw beauty in my hands on that day. I didn't even realize when I stopped worrying about my hands altogether. It felt so beautiful. I had been getting myself worked up for no reason at all. Sometimes, I remember these things and laugh at myself. For those times, I put a lot of energy into worrying when I could occupy myself with exciting things. I was a child, and I am grateful for those incidents. They played very significant roles in my becoming.

Key Points

When you understand the truth that worrying bears no gain for you, you'll quit it for good. Anxiety makes it very difficult, but you are more than capable. You come from a history of women who fought the most significant wars and came out victorious; how could you not win? Winning is in your blood. Below are the key points that you should keep in your heart.

1. Worrying bears no gain for you—quit dwelling in it.

2. Take charge of your worries, don't get worked up for things you cannot change.

3. Anxiety is a common thing for active and intelligent minds. Go easy on yourself.

4. Instead of worrying, why not seek a solution?

5. You are more prominent than anxiety.

My dear black woman, we have come to the end of this chapter. I beg of you, employ what the anxiety chapter taught you into your life. You'd see how much positive change you'd record. Now, let's go on to the next chapter and explore courage!

Chapter Four

Understanding The Concept of Courage

"It is impossible to live without failing at something unless you live so cautiously that you might as well not have lived at all, in which case you have failed by default."
– J. K. Rowling

Courage is another concept I would like you to understand as I help you sail through this ninety-day journey of your life. Courage helps you to overcome fear.

I want to refer to the emotion, fear, as we go through this chapter. Some people believe fear is a virtue because they can benefit from it. Others believe it is not because of past experiences they've had with fear. I will not outrightly categorize fear as a virtue or a vice because it's simply an emotion. It is a natural human response to perceived danger and a critical feeling that can either make or mar a man or woman per se. It is how you deal with the fear that can be considered "virtuous" or not. For courage to exist, fear must be present. Else, courage would not even exist.

What causes fear? You probably are already trying to meander through some of the causes in your mind. Adorable! Well, I'll say fear comes when you perceive there is a threat of harm to you, either physically, emotionally, psychologically, natural, or even imagined. Yes, some people can get so afraid when they think something or someone is out to get them, but in the end, it's all in their imagination. I don't know if you've experienced that before? I'll explain.

As little children, we all had these, should I call them, crazy fears? It sounds a little bit off, though; let's move on. Personally, while growing up, I had a thing against horror movies. Whenever I came across a scary film with ghosts in a dark room or creatures who ate their victims alive all in the dark, my mind would tell me to turn it off, but I would do otherwise.

Yes, I was stubborn. At one point, I wanted to overcome that fear so bad that I stayed up late into the night watching a horror movie. The movie had to do with zombies and the sort. I was shivering under my duvet by the time I finished the movie. The worst part of it all was that I was alone in my room. I tried to get some sleep, but any slight movement or sound I heard or perhaps imagined, would make my eyes snap wide open. I'd cry terribly and blame myself for watching the movie. Yeah, I was that afraid. The fear didn't go away just immediately, but as time passed, I grew older and had this understanding that there was nothing to be scared of as it was just a movie.

I had a friend who never dared to sleep with the lights off. She'd go the extra mile by getting a lamp to light up the room if the lights ever went off. I told her there was nothing to be scared of, but she never believed it. I had to plead with her to try it, and after so many days of constant cajoling, she gave in. Now, she can sleep with lights on or off, and that's a big win for me, I guess. Yay!

Now, enough of the childhood fear stories. Let's get to some real-life adult situations of fear.

Have you ever been called up to stand before a crowd, and you're like, "No, I can't do this. You have to call someone else, please." You're begging whoever it is not to call you up, but they do so regardless, and the whole crowd is waiting and cheering you for you. When you eventually get on stage, you can't say a word at first, and you stand there, snapping your fingers and looking at the vast crowd. Cowering until you find the courage to speak or perform as the case may be. Standing and talking to the public in a situation like that sums up courage.

Cambridge Dictionary defines courage as the ability to control your fear in a dangerous or difficult situation. Even though you may be afraid, it is the choice and willingness to confront agony, pain, danger, uncertainty, or intimidation.

It is okay to feel fear in managing your emotions, but do not let it consume you. Fear can make you miss out on a lot of opportunities. It can hinder your progress in the sense that you were holding back for a long time, something you should have begun from the onset. You're a black woman, and by your color, you are strong. Absurd right? But it would be best if you realized that being black goes way beyond your skin color. It would help if you chose to be in charge of your fear. You will bend it to your desire and not the other way round. I'm not saying this because I want to say it or because it's that easy, far from it. I know how hard it is to overcome fear, but you have to try eventually. You have to start from somewhere, and you have to start now because time waits for no one.

You might be asking, "Where do I start from?" Or "how do I start?" Take a deep breath, begin with the small things. Doing the little things well would make you more courageous to take up the big stuff. Don't you think so, too?

Key Points

Courage is quite an intricate ability to master, but you have to exhibit it to make progress in life, even if it's just the little bits. You need to know your fear, understand it and embrace it. Only then can you overcome it and show courage. Below are the critical points for this section.

1.   Fear is simply an emotion. It is how to deal with the fear that can be considered "virtuous" or not.

2.   In managing your emotions, it is okay to feel fear but not let it consume you.

3.   Some fears are simply imaginary.

4.   It is hard to overcome fears, but you have to try eventually.

5.   Courage is the choice and willingness to confront agony, pain, danger, uncertainty, or intimidation, even though you may be afraid.

What Courage Entails

Courage entails intent and contemplation, personal fear, worthy or virtuous act, and self-endangerment. I want to shred it into bits for you, so let's have this scenario: You have a boyfriend or a husband, and you've been together for a year now. Let's call him Zack. So, Zack used to be all-loving and caring when you started dating until a month ago when he began exhibiting some odd behaviors. He starts staying out late, coming home infrequently, and usually swaying like a palm tree and reeking alcohol. Zack is a shadow of himself, and you're worried. You try to talk to Zack, communicate with him, and ask him what was wrong and why he was the way he is now, but you know what he does? He hits you, and you can't believe what just happened. In the spur of the moment, you want to retaliate, tell him spiteful words and make him realize how much he's hurt you in the past days. You want to scream and cry and yell at him because he's being a jerk, but you're calm, and you don't even know what's happening anymore. You decide to give Zack some time again, but he's grown worse, and the signs are now glaring that he's cheating. He knows you're aware, but he doesn't care, so you decide to call it a wrap, but Zack pleads for another chance. What the hell, right? I know. But you love Zack, and it's blinded you, so you forgive him.

Zack puts up good behavior for some months, and you're thankful that you stayed. It's a month to your second anniversary, and Zack repeats the same behavior. He hits you twice as hard this time, and you have a swollen face and a miscarriage. Now, you've had enough; you sit in your bathtub crying, remembering the good times you shared and how lonely and possibly miserable you would be without him. He's your everything and you don't know what you'd do without him. So you're afraid and at crossroads. You tell your friend, and she tells you to leave him. You say she doesn't understand you. You refuse to believe that Zack never loved you from the onset. You can call him a manipulator if you want. It's your anniversary date, and nothing's changed. You get no show of love even on your special day, but a pale "Happy anniversary," and that's the last straw that breaks the ice. So you take a deep breath and walk up to this monster you once loved and tell him it's over, never to look back.

Touchy story? That's up to you and really but not the point. It's only an illustration of what courage entails. The intent is what you wish to achieve. In this story, you intended to find peace and happiness elsewhere as the relationship was draining you. Contemplation, synonymous with deliberation and consideration, is a deep thought of the possible side effects of what you intend to do. Contemplation, synonymous with reflection and thinking, is a deep thought of the possible side effects of what you intend to do. What did you contemplate while reading the story? On leaving or staying? Giving him time to change? It's all the questions you ask yourself to make your decision. Then there's your fear. A lot of people would rather die than get out of a situation. They might be distressed in their marriages or relationships. Still, they would not leave because of what people say or what they gain from the individual. But it's wrong. What did we say about self-love? Your happiness first, black queen.

Your fear in the story is the fear of being alone because it's been a long time since you were that way. And you wonder how you're going to cope. This fear could be so overwhelming it would shake you till you bend to it, but be strong, and you'll overcome. It gets better in the long run, and you'd be thankful you made that decision. The virtuous act is that you were wise enough to realize that he was out of love with you if he ever was at all and that you'd ridicule yourself if you continue staying. How can a beautiful black queen be mocked in such a manner? You are PRICELESS, don't let anyone put a price on you. Show your worthiness by standing out. Where others choose to remain in toxic relationships or friendships, say NO, my black woman. Say No.

One more thing; self-endangerment. Did you consider the possibilities that could happen when you approached Zack for a breakup? What if he had hit you again and killed you out of anger this time? In meeting him for a discussion as crucial as that, you knew there were going to be risks, but you took them either way. That's what makes you courageous; intentionally committing any act or taking action after thinking despite the risks attached, primarily inspired by a worthy cause, perhaps in the presence of the emotion, fear. That's what courage entails, queen.

Also, more often than not, courage is confused with so many other concepts. These may include confidence, bravery, and fortitude. As they're not the focus of our chapter, I'll distinguish them from courage so you can further understand what courage is and relate to it on a personal level.

According to Wikipedia, Confidence originates from the Latin word, 'fidere,' meaning "to trust"; therefore, having self-confidence is having trust in oneself. So if you raise your hand when the teacher asks three students to volunteer themselves, without informing them of what they're to do, that's confidence. It's you stepping out in front of the class as a volunteer because you've done something like that or something similar before, so you can take a good guess of what it is. But how would you be so assured you can do whatever the teacher asks if you've not stepped out before? That's when courage comes in. As we now know, courage is the quality of mind or spirit that enables you to face difficulty, danger, and pain despite fear. You're the only one who knows the answer in the class, but you've never said a word since you've been in attendance. You're watching the teacher threaten to punish all the students for not knowing it, and with your heart throbbing and threatening to fall off, you raise your hand and speak up. That's courage. Courage is a prerequisite before confidence.

"When you're operating out of courage, you are saying that no matter how you feel about yourself or your opportunities or the outcome, you are going to take a risk and take a step towards what you want. You are not waiting for the confidence to arrive mysteriously." — *Tribe of Mentors.*

Courage and bravery are similar, but bravery is innate or like an instinct. Bravery is facing a dangerous situation without any fear. It's effortless. While courage is seeing a scary thing and acting, even though you're scared. Unlike bravery, courage is for a cause. A brave person can stand up to a bully without a thought. Still, a courageous person considers the reason and thinks it through, deciding to do so in the presence of fear. Being brave is excellent, as well as being courageous.

Last but not least is fortitude. In short and straightforward terms, it is advanced courage-the type of courage a black woman should have in the face of adversity. It is deciding to fight on and not give up despite the travails you may face.

Key Points

Knowing a thing helps a great deal in imbibing that thing. For that reason, I took my time to explain the whole concept of courage to you. Find the critical points for this section below.

1.   When you know what courage entails, you can begin your journey to becoming a better you, a beautiful black woman in total control of her fear. Work with intent and contemplation, personal fear, worthy or virtuous act, and self-endangerment. Master them, and you'll be loving your growth in no time.

2.   Always think your intentions through.

3.   Courage is mental strength.

Knowing The Types Of Courage

There are different types of courage. There's
Physical, Emotional, Intellectual, Social,
Spiritual, and Moral courage, but I want to talk
about only three. I find that their knowledge has
helped me a great deal and will also help you.

Physical Courage

When people think about courage, they get their
minds on physical courage. It involves you
risking discomfort, injury, pain, or even death at
the expense of something more substantial.
Now, this type of courage is so wild that I may
not cover everything exhaustively, but I'll do well
to touch on it as it needs to be.

I know how it feels as a woman to have a visible
scar that makes people ask, "oh dear, how did
you get this?" and stuff like that. That's because I
have a very close friend who told me about the
history of her scar. She was driving past a
building when she noticed it was on fire and
could hear screams and cries for help. They all
sounded like kids, she told me. Know what she
did? You can take a wild guess.

My friend stayed put in the car and called the
fire department. Uh oh, not what you guessed?
Keep reading. Did I mention my friend is so
beautiful? She has this dark skin that glows,
literally. No, she did not want to risk her
beautiful skin, and truthfully, she was scared. I
could see it in her eyes while she narrated her
story. She was asthmatic, so she was scared of
having an attack if she moved to save them. But
minutes passed, 5, and then 10. Then she

panicked. It's hard staying to watch people die and also leaving when you could do something. So she grabbed her inhaler and dashed into the building. The first thing she saw was the dead body, who happened to be the children's mother. She suffered electrocution in her kitchen due to some electrical faults. A fire started. Her children, who happened to be upstairs asleep, woke up a few minutes after the fire had spread to almost all parts of the house.

In summary, my friend could get to the children and get them calm after several burns. She said she saw death knocking at her door. She doesn't even know how she managed to take the children out before she collapsed. It's a real story, and things like that happen every day. Did you know even a little act of exercising takes courage? Even getting up after falling and trying again? Yes, Queen. Lance Armstrong said, "If you worry about falling off the bike, you'd never get on."

This quote reminds me of the times I fell off a bike as a kid while learning to ride. I'd cry and complain to my mother, and she would soothe me, offering to hold the bike while I pedalled. That little act gave me the courage to continue trying. Sometimes you need someone to encourage you, tell you that you can do whatever, you are a true definition of power, and you should never be ashamed of your skin. You are unique, perfect just as you are. I'll be more than happy to encourage you as we continue this journey.

Emotional Courage

Emotional courage has to do with allowing yourself to feel both pleasant and unpleasant emotions without any attachment. There's a secret to outstanding leadership, and I'll let you in on it--Be emotional. Does it sound a bit awkward? Hold on, let me explain.

Most leaders face tremendous challenges. They do not allow themselves to feel; they want to avoid actual vulnerability. But who says letting yourself be emotional makes you weak? Everyone feels, so no one should dictate what you do with your emotions, my dear black queen! You are the pioneer of your life, and you know what's best for you. Open your heart to feel every emotion, but don't let it consume you. That's what makes you stand out, controlling your emotions. Great leaders have emotional courage, a great deal of confidence in themselves, connect with others, and are committed to a greater purpose – all at the same time. Please understand that when I talk about leadership, I'm not only talking about people in large organizations. No. As long as you want to achieve something you care about, you want to move forward, to see yourself grow; you are a leader, so you must allow yourself to feel. The illustration I gave about Zack is also an example of emotional courage. You will let yourself feel the pain, go through it every step of the way, and when you finish crying, you go to the bathroom, wipe your tears and wash your face, put on that makeup, look elegant, and rock that body of yours. Crown it with that heart-stopping smile because there's no way you are going to let what you feel overcome you. It's about having emotional courage--mastering your emotions, remember?

Moral Courage

Moral courage means standing up for what is right. It involves doing the right thing even when it might bring discomfort to you or when the majority does not support it. Martin Luther King, Harriet Tubman, and others who stood up for slaves exhibited great moral courage. My dear black woman, you should stand up for whatever you feel is right. That's how the world can be better.

You probably work at some ministry, and your co-workers cut corners to get extra privileges, and you know what they're doing wouldn't tell well if they get caught. Right now, you're scared of what they would say if you stand up to reprimand them; that's too far even; let's not talk about standing up to them. Not engaging in the act is a massive move in itself!

One Friday morning, you walk up to where they're discussing their spoils and be like, "I guess you know you're doing the wrong things? It is clearly against our ethics, Ma'ams and Sirs. I think you should stop whatever you're doing, or else I'll make a report to the boss." Suddenly you hear a loud clap from your audience, followed by the rest doing the same. You have just made a "ridiculously wonderful" speech. All your co-workers make jest of you and refuse to take you seriously. Instead, they make fun of you and laugh hard. They fail to acknowledge the truth. But deep inside of them, they know it.

But then you go back to your seat and realize that you're not dead, didn't catch a cold, not paralyzed, probably a few heartbeats out of place, but now you're lovely and much better with a burden off your chest. It's that simple! Never forget, one thing about moral courage is that it is very close to the truth.

Do you want to be morally courageous? The truth should always be in your mouth, and you must be ready to burst out when need be. May I also remind you that being morally courageous is not confined to religion? Yes, remember this always.

Key Points

1.   When people think about courage, they get their minds on physical courage.

2.   Sometimes, you need someone to encourage you and tell you that you can do whatever; you are a true definition of power and should never be ashamed of your skin. You are amazingly perfect, just as you are.

3.   But who says letting yourself feel makes you weak? It doesn't.

4.   When you finish crying, you go to the bathroom, wipe your tears and wash your face, put on that makeup, look elegant, and rock that body of yours. Crown it with that heart-stopping smile because there's no way you are going to let what you feel overcome you.

We have come to the end of the courage chapter!
I hope you enjoyed reading it and finding
strength in it as much as I did while writing it.

Courage is one of the most extraordinary things
you can know. Embrace it wholly and deeply.
The next chapter would be all about love and
broken hearts. Have you loved before, ever
experienced heartbreak? Read on; let's talk
about it all!

Chapter Five

Breakups and Broken Hearts

"Cry. Forgive. Learn. Move on. Let your tears water the seeds of your future happiness."
– Steve Maraboli

I'm excited to talk to you about this topic because I have a lot to say about it. Thankfully, you now understand the concepts of negative emotions, self-love, anxiety, and courage. I advise that you read the chapter on Self-Love as many times as you wish because it's a critical factor in mending your broken heart. The others are important, of course.

The concept of love is undeniably quite abstract and very difficult to describe. The fact that love can find expression in many ways makes it even more complicated. But to make this chapter easy to understand, I'd like us to focus on a straightforward definition of love, that is, a deep attachment or affection for another. When we fall in love, our brain embraces 'happy' chemicals, which it makes by itself. But after a breakup or death of a loved one, they stop being produced, and the body suffers from it, leading to a broken heart. A broken heart is a metaphor for the intense emotional stress you feel when experiencing great and deep longing. I know firsthand how difficult and painful it is to deal with a broken heart. I have two experiences to share, and even though they may not be the same with whatever you're facing or faced in the past, I'll share them still. I want you to know that I understand when you say you're heartbroken.

Five years ago happened to be one of the most challenging years I've ever faced. It was the year my grandma died, and I don't know if you'd say she's "just your grandma," but it was different for me, as it is with most people. She had this illness episode, and I travelled home to be by her side. She didn't want to go to a care home, so I took care of her during that period. It was draining, but I loved her with everything in me and was ready to do anything to make sure she was completely okay. I paid a doctor for home-based medical care, making sure he checked on her every day as well. For weeks she was sick until she started recovering, and I would say with all pride that I was the happiest person in this world. You know, there's always this happiness we feel understanding our loved ones are there, and we can see them, we can touch them, these things might look small sometimes, but I've learned not to take it for granted. I had these long talks I used to have with her immediately. She recovered, and we did all the fun stuff we always did. But it was only two days after she recovered, and I was in the living room calling her to come down for breakfast, that she died. It broke me.

I do not know which hurt more, the fact that a week after, my boyfriend of a year plus posted a picture of his new girlfriend on his social media page. Yeah, he left without any explanation. No words, nothing at all. It hurt the most because he was with the type of girl he had always liked. I knew this because he always talked about her. I was too blind to see the signs, and I paid dearly for it. We'll talk more about this, but let's go back to my grandma's death.

I had these episodes of sobbing, rage, and despair. I was at my lowest. I'd stay up all night and think about why my grandma had to die at that time and why my boyfriend left without any explanation. You could call me a glutton, but at that time, I betrayed everything, my food, my sleep, even my hygiene. It was so bad that my broken heart would often cause my body to secrete high-stress hormones, resulting in severe panic attacks. But I didn't care anymore. I even wished for death.

With a broken heart, I went through the five stages of grief: denial, anger, bargaining, depression, and acceptance. It's funny how at first, after my grandma died, I still went up to her room for an entire week, desperately hoping that I would find her awake on her bed like old times. But it was just my mind refusing to accept the fact that she was gone forever. And my boyfriend? I texted him immediately and asked what was going on. But he outright said that I was simply a rebound, a freaking rebound for over a year. It hurt that much, but the pain didn't go away immediately. Nope, I asked to see him, and he declined. After several pleas, he gave in and explained to me that he had made up with his x-months ago. So, he did not only use me, he had been cheating on me, and I couldn't see the signs. It's also funny when I think of it now because then I thought I was foolish to love. But time made me understand that I didn't need to change who I was because of someone who didn't deserve me in the first place.

After he confessed to me about everything, I stopped living in denial. Then, I became furious. I was so pissed at life for taking away someone I loved and pissed at myself for being "foolish," like I said in the previous paragraph. I was angry at him for taking me for a fool, I was mad at everybody, and my social life became a total mess. I wondered what I was doing because I seemed to lose track of time. I was unrecognizable, always angry, self-loathing, and unforgiving. I contemplated begging my ex to take me back. I did it, but it was a waste of time. Then I opted for suicide, although I never carried it out. I never mustered enough courage to carry out my suicide plans. Then I became numb. Fast forward to six weeks later, and I was not in the least better. This time, I had begun to feel, but it was all the negative feelings I didn't wish to handle, and I became the depressed fellow around that people got used to me being like that. You could never see me smile or laugh; I just wore a long face all day.

The day I decided to go for therapy was rather chucklesome. One of my friends walked up to me, slapped me hard across the cheek, and said, "you're not going to die alone and depressed; come with me." And I started seeing a therapist who helped me a great deal. It took me over a year of reorganization and recovery to reduce the intensity of my grief, but it was worth it every day.

Key Points

1.   Love is a deep attachment or affection for another, a parent, child, or friend.

2.   The five stages of grief are denial, anger, bargaining, depression, and acceptance.

3.   When rejection is involved, shame sets in

4.   Continuous, uncontrollable, and distressing intrusive thoughts are often a component of grieving.

Is It a Broken Heart?

Like approaches to heartbreak vary, it looks different on everyone because it is a form of grief. We all grieve differently. If you've lost a partner, my dear black woman, probably due to death or they walked away, or maybe you even had to walk away, I understand the grief that follows. It's so unbearable. Because you're not just grieving over their loss but your dreams for a future that includes that person. This kind of grief can cause emotional and physical pain. Did you know that many heartbreak symptoms overlap with other disorders, especially depression? And trust me, it's far worse for people who have been previously depressed because a heartbreak could trigger an episode.

As a beautiful black woman on a journey to master her emotions, you should know when you've passed the line of sadness and fallen into depression which is a sign of a broken heart. It starts from losing appetites like I once had, nausea, indigestion, overeating, diarrhea, excessive weight gain, or loss. Other signs could be insomnia, bad dreams, lack of energy, restlessness, weakness, body pains, and exhaustion. Never dismiss these as the usual stuff, and it is your body and soul whispering their fatigue and pain.

In relationship breakups, the affected ones usually turn their anger over the rejection toward themselves. Yes, just like I did. I am thankful that this happened to me, so I can relate precisely to all of these as I go on this journey with you. It's beautiful now that I've overcome that phase.

When you can't think about anything else but sit all day and let your ex or dead one run through your mind, it's time to reassess, queen. Self-hate can deepen your depression, beautiful woman, and cause narcissistic wounding. The process of self-attack can range from mild self-doubt to critical self-recrimination or accusation, which is sure to leave a lasting imprint on your self-worth. I beg of you not to let it get to this extent. In this phase, it's eaten deep into you. It is on the verge of taking your self-worth and causing you to doubt your ability to love, personality-efficacy, attachment worthiness, ability to move on, everything, queen, everything.

I've shared a big part of me with you in this chapter. I am glad that I could. Do you think you're in the last phase of self-hate? Let's do a quick assessment test. Do you feel like life isn't worth living without the other person? You feel worthless, right? Possibly, even angry at yourself for some of your decisions? Or mad at life because it took someone you cared about? Alright. Whatever your answer is, write it down on paper; we're heading somewhere. The first step, remember, is knowing the signs.

When you find yourself avoiding your friends, my gorgeous black woman, you've got to pause and rethink things. I know how unbelievably difficult it can be to maintain friendships in the wake of a significant breakup. Still, you have to wait for real this time. Please don't take it out on them. Your friends and family are the only ones who'll stand by you when you can't even hold yourself up anymore. So don't push them away. It's okay to explain to them that you do not want company for the time being but don't be out for too long. Talk to them, cry if you're okay with it, and let them offer you comfort. It's part of your healing process.

Finding closure and struggling with boundaries is another sign you shouldn't look past. Oh my, trust me when I say it's damn hard, but you know yourself. You know now that you should love yourself so much, so work, toil all day and try to break past that bad habit of stalking your ex on social media. I understand that pain can make you behave in ways you ordinarily wouldn't, like publishing passive-aggressive posts. That's a red flag, and I want you to be smart enough to notice it. It's only fueling your anger and resentment. You don't also have to block them forever; just let yourself feel, then purge. If you're also thinking of ways to "bump" into them and try to get things working again, you have to stop. Did you break up with them? Think about why you did and remember that you should be courageous and watch how you'd scale through this stage, totally refined. Oh, they broke up with you? It's fine. Their loss and that's on period. You are everything a woman should entail; you are strong and black, so why cry all night and refuse to move on when your ex failed to acknowledge your value. A therapist would tell you this, a good friend would do the same, and I'll let you know the same. It's time, queen, get up.

Last but not least, post-traumatic stress disorder. This disorder is mainly about the inability of a person to recover after experiencing a terrifying event. It may last months or years, with triggers that can bring back memories of the trauma accompanied by intense emotional and physical reactions. Heartbreaks are also known to trigger PTSD. So if you are a PTSD patient, you'd need this book to understand your emotions, master and take care of them. Watch out for the ninety-day plan!

Key Points

1. Heartbreak looks different for everyone because it is a form of grief, and we all grieve differently.

2. When you can't think about anything else but sit all day and let your ex or dead one run through your mind, it's time to reassess.

3. Self-loathe eats deep into you and takes away your self-worth and ability to love.

4. Look for the signs. Are you avoiding friends or struggling in your business?

5. Are you stalking? That's a big no-no.

It's Time To Move On

I wondered how some people moved on so quickly. One of my friends didn't care when his girl broke up with him, which added to my self-doubt. But did you know that everyone has their coping mechanisms? I realized this quite late when I was so depressed that I attended therapy sessions. While many cry all night and wallow in despair and get better, some don't come out of it, and a few repress their feelings, trying not to face the pain. Still, in the end, it eventually leads to panic, anxiety, or depression. Others slip into addiction and rebound relationships to deal with a broken heart. All these are the different ways people deal with broken hearts, but you should deal with a broken heart like a queen for a black woman, and I'll show you how.

I was hoping you could take out the journal I asked you to write on the cause of your pain and how you feel. Now is the time to deal with your emotions, like the strong woman you are. Ready?

The first step is allowing yourself to feel your feelings, and I believe you know what that means from the previous chapters we went through together? With emotional shock, you have to be gentle with yourself and feel your feelings. Don't inflict bodily harm to yourself. Do you think you're at fault? But what if you aren't, and it's just guilt clouding your senses and eating you up? You aren't a robot, and your feelings are there for a reason—they can help you move through difficult experiences, but only if you release them. During this process, validate your feelings by saying things like "I accept I'm experiencing this emotion." or "I'm feeling this way."

Next is cutting off communication with your ex if it's about a breakup. Remember those 'happy' emotions I talked about in an earlier section? I know how much you want to feel them again, how much you crave them, but you'll undoubtedly struggle to move on if you go back to your ex. You broke up with them, so why bend to your craving? They'll eventually dissolve, and you won't even remember them. I advocate for cutting your ex off immediately, but not forever. They still have an atom of humanity in them, or don't they? So if you feel it's okay to check in on them once in a while, it's lovely. Just don't let it become the norm.

Finding a support system is also a step to moving on. And that's why I told you not to push your friends away. I hope you smile as you read this upon realizing that you need people around you. No man is an island, gorgeous one! So pick up that phone and call whoever comes to your mind, no, not your ex, not the one you're getting away from, but those who will fill you with nothing but positivity and warmth. Right now is the time you need people the most. Don't deceive yourself that no one cares about you. Many people love you and want to support you, but how can they when you don't tell them? Who knows, they might have gone through exactly what you're going through and are ready to hold your hand and walk you through every stage. Give it a try.

Hey beautiful black woman, are you still with your journal? We're about to do an exercise.

Okay, so you know why you broke up or were broken up with, right? It doesn't matter if you're not sure why they broke up with you. All you're going to do is write a list of your ex's negative aspects, take a deep breath, and look at it. Whenever you feel like going back, flip back to the page and focus on counterbalancing your obsessive thinking with this mental exercise. Avoid thinking that there's something wrong with you. I did just that for weeks, and that's why the healing process was slow. But despite that, don't judge the length of your healing process. I'm different from you, and you're different from me. Stop wondering why you've not gotten over that six months relationship because it all depends on how attached you were to the person.

Take care of yourself, make sure to exercise, eat good food, and breathe. Also, try as much as you can to build a good sleep routine. It helps in fighting your negative emotions. Create new habits, make plans, find all your interests, whether old or new. It's about developing you. Accept that closure is something you may need to find on your own. If your ex did not explain why he left you, you have to create your healthy narrative, but consider seeing a therapist if it doesn't help. If the breakup triggers your PTSD, you must seek outside help. Trust that the pain won't last forever; believe that this too shall pass. Reflect on the positive things. Embrace the excitement of new possibilities and remind yourself of your awesomeness! No matter how difficult it might seem at first, believe me when I say you'd love again and heal. Give yourself time. The healing will come.

Key Points

1.   A few people repress their feelings, trying not to face the pain. Still, in the end, it eventually leads to panic, anxiety, or depression.

2.   Feel, but don't become your feelings.

3.   How would your loved ones know if you don't communicate?
4.   Counterbalance your obsessive thoughts with a list of your ex's opposing sides.

5.   Take care of yourself and find closure with yourself.

My dear black woman, we have reached the end of this chapter! I hope you had a lot of fun in it. Now, come with me; let's explore contentment in the next chapter. It'll be fun, I promise you.

Chapter Six

Contentment

"Fortify yourself with contentment, for this is an impregnable fortress."
--Epictetus

That last chapter was quite the chapter. It stirred a lot of emotions, I know. This chapter is self-explanatory, so it'll be a bit shorter and provide warmth to you. Let's begin. Shall we?

Contentment is being satisfied with what you have. You have a friend who has at least three gowns from all the popular clothing brands, Old Navy. Reuters, House Of Versace, Burberry, Chanel, Gucci, name it! This friend flaunts them all to your face because you have just three gowns from unpopular brands. You don't pay any heed to her, but you rock the outfits you own in all pride and glamor. That's some high level of contentment shit. You're joyful with what you own. It doesn't mean you're not aiming higher. It a just that you're not getting caught up in sadness because of the things you are yet to own.

It takes contentment to be happy with the little thing you possess and not get jealous about the possessions of others. Instead of doing that, please take it as motivation and work hard for self-improvement. I have a friend I tell about my financial progress. I've never seen anyone so genuinely happy for another as much as this friend of mine. Even at his lowest, he would call me to congratulate me on any feat I achieved. It gladdens me so much, not having to feel guilty about my wins or anything.

Some friends can't tell certain things about you, especially your wins, because they'd get jealous, and it always shows even when they try to hide it. From the side comments or mutterings to avoidance, all because you're not happy about the person's growth. As a contented person, you'll be great.

If you are a student and don't have the luxury to live as wealthy as most of your friends, contentment is one key attribute you need to imbibe to scale through college. Contentment keeps you happy and helps you push harder in life. It's not just in college.

As a black woman who is courageous enough to go on this journey with me, I need you to understand that your peace of mind should come first no matter what. Contentment is among the virtues that can offer you that. It would bring positivity and self-love for self-improvement. It allows you to be ambitious and aspire for a better future; it restricts you from greed and gives peace to your present. If you aren't at peace with what you achieved by yourself, how can you be motivated to work toward a better future?

Another reason you should be content is to know what it is to be truly happy. If you're at peace with yourself and your achievements, happiness will find its way into your life with ease. Do not live a sad and monotonous life because you do not own all you desire. You'll regret it if you do.

From the things you own, create your kind of life. It dawns on me that humans do not need so much to have a great life every day. No, I'm not trying to make you see reasons why you shouldn't indulge in luxury. I'm only trying to inform you that it is vital that you enjoy life with the little you own while you wait for the big things to come. Also, you need to master the difference between your needs and your wants.

We all have our needs and wants, and I'm sure yours would differ from mine. While I could be desirous of a helicopter of my own, do I need it? Contentment would help me distinguish between my wants and my needs. I need the necessities of life, food, shelter, and clothing to survive in this world. But if I let my greed take over and spend my money every time on mere wants without considering my needs, I may end up begging for food or a roof over my head. You're a pretty woman, and you want to stay pretty, I understand. But first, you have to consider your money at hand. If it'll see you through your needs without you feeling the brunt of it, that's wonderful. You have to cut down on some wants and invite contentment into your heart if it won't. Always fulfil the needs first as they are the necessities. The desires are secondary.

One other importance that you need to remember always is simplicity. We're on a journey through emotional self-care, and what's better than being able to relieve yourself of that thought and take a deep breath in, say to yourself that "you've got this!" Because if you don't, who else would? A content person is a simple person, and that's a fantastic trait. She doesn't have to go around nursing ill feelings because she can't get something she wants at the moment or because of her friends' success. You have to note this beautiful trait because it is critical to self-love and genuine happiness, as simple as it may look. Practice gratitude, assure yourself every day the fact that nothing is permanent and that material things do not often promote long-term happiness.

I watched a short clip some time ago about how satisfying a want would only make you develop another. Mind you, and I'm not asking you not to indulge a desire when you can afford to, not at all. I need you to understand that you shouldn't base your happiness on material things. Happiness should come from within, realizing that you are a perfect creation and that no one can love you better than yourself. Life is not a race or competition. A friend of mine gives me gifts from time to time. I accept them with so much gratitude and sincere happiness, and I'd say to him, "you motivate me to work harder every day." And that's from a place of genuine love. I'm thankful for my present, and I know my future will be better because I'm working towards that with contentment as a weapon.

Key Points

1.   Contentment doesn't stop you from improving.

2.   If you're at peace with yourself and your achievements, happiness will find its way into your life with a lot of ease.

3.   Life is not a race or competition.

Are You Contented?

I know I've been talking about contentment a lot, and you keep saying, "Alright, I've heard what you said contentment is about, but I'm still unsure if I got what it takes." Please read this section well, as it covers a few qualities needed to achieve contentment.

Quick question: Are you satisfied? Satisfaction is a significant attribute of contentment. When you're content, you'll be okay with what you have and happy for others who are progressing. Did you know? Contented people regard the possession of others as entirely usual because they believe it is only a matter of time before they can legally get their own. They never give way for the lust for wealth to affect them negatively.

Get that envy out of your system. To envy is to have negative thoughts over someone else's achievement. On your journey to being contented, my dear queen, many people will celebrate and call you to join in their celebration. Gladly accept their invitation if you have the time to spare and let yourself feel genuine happiness for them. I want to state that feeling envious of someone who got their wealth through illegal means is very wrong. Personally, it doesn't sit well with me. Why would you envy someone you have no idea of what they have been through to reach that level? Focus on your growth. People are different, and so is their growth period. Write out your achievements in your journal when you feel jealous of someone's growth and pat yourself on the back. You're doing great!

When I realize how greedy and desperate some people can be, I shiver in my bones. They can be so desperate to the extent of committing great moral evils, like human trafficking, murder, theft, and the likes. They're never satisfied, always wanting more; that's greed. On your way to being a better version of yourself, you have to take away avarice from yourself. It will help you build trust between you and your colleagues, friends, and family. Contented people have a passionate hatred for greed.

Content people hate corruption. Corruption is any dishonest or fraudulent conduct. Bribery, extortion, fraud, abuse of power, embezzlement, etc., are examples of corrupt practices which people engage in to meet their wants. Yes, wants. Content people are careful to avoid all forms of corruption, and you beautiful black woman should do so too.

The last one I'd talk about is humility. It is the quality of being modest—the liberation from your consciousness and a form of temperance that does not involve pride or self-deprecation. Humble people know their self-worth; they understand their strengths but do not dwell too much on them or announce to everyone about them.

I love this attribute because it helps one get true friends most of the time. When people know you're humble and not one to boast, they'd always want to be around you.

Over the years, I've watched many discontent people reveal their discontentment, which always harms our society. It's like an ill wind that blows community no good. Lack of contentment has served as an ambassador for major moral vices and promoted the culture of greed, corruption, engagement in criminal acts, the prevalence of immorality, and so on. We're all working on our emotions and, in the long run, giving back to society by spreading good around. Still with your journal? Here's a to-do list for you:

– Count your blessings
– Practice kindness
– Let go of what I can't control
– Listen to my heart
– Be productive yet calm
– Just breathe

It's elementary, and you'd get used to it as you repeat it every day. You don't have to follow it as it is; feel free to explore your choices. Good luck being content.

Key Points

1.   Satisfaction is a crucial attribute to contentment.

2.   Get that envy out of your system.

3.   On your way to being a better version of yourself, you have to take away greed.

4.   Content people hate corruption.

Phew! It's been one hell of a journey. Tell me, love, did you enjoy this chapter? Did everything I wrote about contentment in this chapter strike a chord? Have you been a discontented person? It's okay. The good thing is you have the power and knowledge you need to begin your contentment journey at this very moment. I hope you bask in contentment and revel in its goodness. Now, let's start the next chapter! It's all about self-worth.

Chapter Seven

Self-Worth Through a Black Woman's Lenses

Because one believes in oneself, one doesn't try to convince others. Because one is content with oneself, one doesn't need others' approval. Because one accepts oneself, the whole world accepts him or her.
—*Lao Tzu.*

Self-worth is one virtue that all of us should possess. What is self-worth? It is simply the value you see in yourself. It is that self-pride that glows in you with so much brilliance. Self-worth is what stands you out from the crowd.

For you to stand out in this world, you need a tremendous amount of self-worth. You must know one thing. Your self-worth is a significant determinant of how much people think you are worth. And that plays a vital role in how they would treat you. For this reason, you must wear self-worth like it is your armour. It is one of the most beautiful things you can do for yourself. I learned about self-worth very early in my life, and it helped me immensely. When you fail to define your worth, the world will define it for you. I've never met women who express their worth as much as black women do. Black women do not accept stupidity and poor treatment because they know what they are worth. It would help if you first valued yourself for people to see your value.

I've also met some black women who let people push them around because they do not know what they are worth. When I was in university, I had this gorgeous and intelligent friend named Marilyn. She's one of the most innovative women I've met all my life. The whole class was always in awe of her. Going by this, you'd expect Marilyn to be a girl full of confidence, right? But the reverse was the case with my dear Marilyn. If poor self-worth were human, it would have been Marilyn. She was blind to all the wonders we saw in her. Who wouldn't love such gorgeousness and intelligence in one person? She'd second guess everything and always question if she was worthy of honour. At first, I thought she was just a humble girl. But as time progressed, I found out that she had a very little sense of self-worth.

She'd condone a lot of silly behavior just because she thought she wasn't all that important. I need you to know one thing. The moment people notice that you have minimal self-worth, they'd make it littler by taking you through every shitty thing. My friend, there are lots of Marilyns in this world. People who dazzle yet are unaware of the spark they bear. I am sure that you are curious about what happened to Marilyn. Aren't you? Well, it ended well. She spent quite a lot of time revelling in her poor sense of self-worth. I don't know precisely how or when, but I remember Marilyn suddenly changing from the timid and weak girl into a powerful and bold girl sometime later at school. With Marilyn, I realized something. Black women are at their prettiest when they are aware of themselves and their power. Nothing comes close to the power of a black woman who knows her self-worth. They are the kind of black women that change the world and cause people to marvel. Don't you want to be that kind of strong woman? I know you do.

Many people work hard at making black women see their self-worth through distorted lenses. This class of people is always afraid of the strength of black women. So, they try to make them small by messing with their sense of self-worth. My dear black woman, the truth is, you'd meet a lot of people who would question yourself and all of your abilities. You'd get the good things you deserve and find yourself wondering if you deserve them or not. You'd find yourself in high places and ask yourself if the apex is made for you too. The era when people intimidated black women and made their self-worth into playthings is long gone. In this era, black women wear their self-worth with all the pride in the world. I am more than glad to be born at this time. Tell me, aren't you happy, too?

It would help if you prepared yourself to encounter the people who might make you feel terrible about yourself and your life. Sometimes, preparing yourself for things enables you to respond to them better. You know, people do not learn how to fight on the battlefield. No matter the intimidation such people would try to make you feel, do not give in.

Never stop to ponder on what they would tell you. Instead, pay no mind to all the manipulations they bear by focusing on all the goodness you carry. Yes, I know it is not an easy thing to do. I know how difficult it is not to pay attention to negative people. You know what? I find it crazy that we listen to negativity more than positivity. If we can be so keen on listening to people who say terrible things about us, why can't we do the same when it comes to the good stuff? Well, it is human nature. But, I trust in your abilities to never let what people say or do reduce your self-worth. When I get overwhelmed sometimes, I draw strength from the first line of a quote by Virginia Woolf. It says:

'I feel a thousand capacities spring up in me.'

Whenever I perceive that my self-worth is suffering, I remind myself of all my capacities with this quote. It is one of my favourites. I hope it strengthens you too. Do not give any space for the diminishing of your worth.

Key Points

1. A great sense of your self-worth is one of the best things you can ever have.

2. Nothing has the right to make you feel less of yourself.

3. If you do not define your self-worth, other people will do it for you. They most likely won't describe it the way you want them to.

4. You'd meet people who would try to destroy your self-worth at some point in

your life. But, you are more than powerful enough to overpower them.

5. You need a tremendous amount of self-worth to excel in this life.

Walk Away When They Begin To Shrink You

Many people deal with poor self-worth today because they do not know how to walk away. No, I'm not talking about taking pleasant walks in pretty boulevards. I'm talking about walking away from people who make your self-worth a mess, people who make you feel bad about yourself. They are the worst kind of people anyone can call a friend. They do not only make your self-worth terrible, but they also make you conform to things that are beneath you. You won't even realize it until you're fully into poor self-worth.

I've had quite a lot of friends in my life. Now, I have just a few of them. I was that one friend that could go to extreme lengths for anyone I called a friend. I do not mean to brag, but I was an angel. That friend that people always wished they had. Somehow, I attract people to myself effortlessly. Making friends and connecting with people is one thing that has always come easy to me. I like to think that I would have been an expert in my field by now if I had spent the energy I put into making friends on networking. You know, it is no cliché when people say your network is your net worth. But I do not blame myself so much now. I was young; I saw the world in rose-tinted glasses. Just like I've had many friends, I've made a couple of mistakes in friendships. I thought it was cool to keep everyone around me. I never knew the importance of filtering friendship circles. A terrible lesson awakened that need in me. You want to know what it was, don't you? I'll share it with you, my dear. I write this book to empower you, and learning from my experience can do that too.

I metamorphosed from a boisterous youth into an afraid and shy teenager. It amazed my parents a lot. Oh, how reclusive I became. I used to be among those who never believed people could influence them. I can hear my younger self saying, 'no one in this life can influence me. I am strong' as I write this book. I didn't even know when I was under the influence of the friends I swore could never influence me. I think it started with them saying I was too loud and everywhere. They didn't like it that I was as audacious as I was. I tried to please them by shutting away some of my capacities. It took me a long time to know. Knowing was quite tricky for me. People with problems sometimes refuse to see that they have issues. It was that way with me too. I couldn't just believe it nor accept it. I had to do a lot of self-examinations first. Girl, I felt so miserable!

Sometimes, we all make this mistake. We stick with people that diminish our self-worth without even realizing it. We only know it after a lot of damage must have been done. I have experienced it, and I know how it feels perfectly well. This experience made me begin to undertake a personal evaluation at intervals. I think it is something that you would love to adopt, too, for the sake of your personal growth and self-worth. From time to time, take a pause and evaluate yourself and the level of your self-worth. Doing this doesn't only make you a better woman; it also helps you retrace your steps quickly the very moment you begin to stray.

Mistakes are easier to correct with early discovery.
When you discover your mistake, please don't beat yourself up about it too much. Of course, it is perfectly normal to feel wrong about such a thing. Instead of spending a lot of time boasting over it, take your time and study your mistakes. All the places you went wrong. Don't ever deceive yourself by thinking that no one has the power to influence your self-worth. My dear, people are much more potent than they believe they are. Don't permit anyone to make you a mess by ignoring them when they trample on your priceless self-worth.

Do you know one other primary reason why people get afraid when it comes to walking out on people that shrink them? It is friendship and family. You know, the people that will diminish your self-worth are not strangers most of the time. You'd find them among your friends and family members. I have come to learn that humans love to make excuses and tolerate a lot of crazy stuff when it involves their loved ones. I am guilty of it, too. Don't feel bad.

I'll be laconic at this point. My dear black woman, you have to master the art of walking away from people and the things the moment they begin to shrink you. Nothing in this world is worth your self-worth. No matter how good a thing is, you really can't enjoy it with poor self-worth. Walking away may be crazy at first, but it is worth it. Sometimes, you'd feel like you're alone at the end of the world, like all you have is just yourself. In the future, you'll see that walking away from everything that shrinks you and your self-worth is one of the best things you can ever do for yourself.

Key Points

1. Nothing in this world is worth your self-worth.

2. To have the beautiful and sweet life you desire, you have to master the art of walking away from anything that shrinks you.

3. You are powerful enough to walk away. You are much stronger than you know.

4. Forgive yourself for all the times you let people mess with your self-worth.

Embrace Self-Improvement

Sometimes, lack triggers poor self-worth in people. I'm not talking about the lack of material things in the shortage that springs from the inside. For example, staying in a room full of intellectuals and having nothing meaningful to say during discussions is one great kind of lack. You'd most likely feel less of yourself. You might begin to weep and hate those people simply because you do not measure up to their standards. That would be one hell of an adverse reaction. Instead of reacting negatively to the situation, how about trying something different?

When feelings of inadequacy trigger your self-worth, the first thing you should do is identify. Sit your ass down and go through a self-valuation. Try as much as possible to remember every single thing that reduces your self-worth. Knowing the problem always makes it easier and faster to get a solution. I know you're curious now. After identification, what comes next? Or, is that where it all ends? Certainly not. When you finish identifying the things that make you feel less important, embrace self-improvement. Self-improvement comes in different forms. When it comes to feelings of inadequacies like not having enough skill, poor growth, and the likes, don't waste your time by wallowing in self-pity and crying about the situation. Stand up and improve yourself. Take courses, learn from mentors, do research, and share your ideas. These things might seem easy to do now, but they are not. They require a lot of dedication, time, and most importantly, the zeal and willingness to improve yourself. You'd be amazed at how much your self-worth would shoot up by the time you improve yourself. Not only does it make your voice bolder, but it also makes you open to better opportunities.

Sometimes, our poor self-worth arises from things we have no control over. It could be the way we look, speak, the family we come from, scars, race, and many others. I had a classmate who talked with a lisp back in the day. Almost everyone in the class always laughed whenever this particular student spoke. We were kids who didn't fully realize the damage those giggles, peals of laughter, and side talks caused. The student was brilliant, but she was quick to recoil into her shell because of our laughter. Writing about this now, I feel terrible for what other classmates and I did to that girl. We never give her space to shine. Also, we never got to learn from her because we were too busy. We only had time to make fun of her unique accent. As I grew older, I learned to embrace people more. It also dawned on me that the differences we share give the world its beauty. Nothing creates beauty more than variety.

If you're like this classmate I used to have, I need you to know that it is perfectly normal to feel wrong about these things. But what isn't okay is allowing the things you have no control over control your own life. You have to master acceptance. Acceptance, in this case, is serious self-improvement. You might need to do some work on your self-worth by standing up for yourself and refusing to allow anyone to silence

you for any reason. It is not an easy thing to do,
but the very moment you step out of silence is
the moment you teach people not to ridicule you.

Take your time and improve yourself in the areas
needed. Then, accept yourself for the things that
you cannot undo. Never fail to remind yourself
that you are lovely in all your elements.

Key Points

Embrace self-improvement and see how your
self-worth would improve significantly. Start
with a tiny step at a time. A lot of small steps
make the significant steps. Remember this every
day.
Find the critical points for this section below.

1. Embrace self-improvement with all that
   you are.
2. It is okay to feel inadequate. What is not
   okay is wallowing in it.
3. Self-improvement makes your voice
   bolder and louder.
4. Do not gloat over your inadequacies.
   Focus on working on yourself instead.
5. Self-improvement increases self-worth.

My dear black woman, we have come to the end
of this chapter. I hope you get enough value from
it. The next chapter will be all about depression
and its elements. Let's dig in!

Chapter Eight

Depression And Its Elements

I found that with depression, one of the most important things you could realize is that you're not alone.
—Dwayne Johnson

Depression is one illness that many people do not like to talk about despite affecting a considerable percentage of humanity. Before I go on with this topic, I would first talk about the meaning of depression.

So, what is depression? A lot of people begin to think about grief and sadness. No, depression is deeper than that. Although, grief and sadness are elements of depression. Do you know the difference? I'll explain to the best of my ability with a concise story.

Losing people and things I hold close to my heart is one thing that scares me to my bones in this life. We all want people to be with us forever—such beautiful wishful thinking. People will always come and go like the seasons. One of the most challenging phases of my life came when I was twenty years old. I feel teary writing about it now. Somehow, the grief never really goes away.

It just hides somewhere and comes out on days you least expect. So, I lost my boyfriend to death in a car accident when I was twenty. It felt like a wild dream. My brain and body went numb with shock and deep sadness. For days, I'd lock myself in and weep until I lost all my strength. It felt like it was the end of the world for me. I'd look through the pictures we took together, relive the magical kisses, sniff his shirts, and cry. On some days, I wished to go back in time to hug him tighter and love him harder. But time travel happens only in science fiction, right?

My boyfriend's death affected me for quite a long time, and I began to think I was depressed. After I had healed from the loss, I realized I mistook my grief and sadness for depression. It is normal to grieve when bad things happen to us. It is our sorrow finding expression. But depression doesn't work like this. It just hits you like a tornado. Depression can come to you for no reason. It can envelop you and hold you intensely even if you are not grieving about anything. Do you get the difference between depression and sadness now? I hope you do.

Depression comes in varying degrees. Sometimes, a whiff of it hits you for a short time, and you bounce back quickly. Other times, it rents a room inside you and refuses to go. Either short or long time, depression is still depression. Do you know the signs of depression? The commonest of them all is the sudden and

absolute loss of interest in things that used to set your heart on fire. You have to note that this is different from taking a break. I'll use myself as an example. I am a writer who thrives in writing. But I take a break from writing sometimes. It gets overwhelming. I accept these breaks to keep my head above water and observe everything around me more keenly. Not only does this increase my creativity, but it also keeps me from losing touch with my environment.
In the case of depression, I'd dislike writing and lose interest in it. It'll no longer intrigue me like it used to. Do you get the drift now? Depression involves a total loss of interest.

It would interest you to know that almost everyone goes through depression at some point in a lifetime. What does this mean? It means depression is an illness, just like any other. But the crazy thing is that people shy away from talking about depression and supporting people that suffer it. There are a lot of misconceptions and wrong knowledge about depression in our society. Some people hold the belief that depression is the work of some demon. Some believe that depression is the fate of evil people. These things make me shake my head and laugh in sorrow. There is so much to unlearn about depression in society. If you're among the group of people who have wrong ideas of depression, I hope this book helps you unlearn. It is a gradual process, but you can go through it if you set your heart to it. Remember, there is nothing that you cannot do if you're determined. As you unlearn, do not hesitate to educate the people around you. Depressed people would get more help and support the more people become enlightened. You want that to happen, don't you? I know you do! So, make it all easier by doing your bit.

Key Points

Depression is one illness that a lot of people demonize so much. I am thrilled to talk to you about depression in this book. Find the critical points for this session below.

1. Depression is not taboo, do not be ashamed if you are depressed.

2. Depression, grief, and sadness are very different things. Knowing the difference between them would help you so much.

3. Depression is not the punishment one gets for being evil; neither is it the work of some demon. It is a mental illness that can happen to the best of us.

4. Depression is not the end of your life.

There Is No Shame In Seeking Help

Many depressed people die in silence every day because they think getting depressed is a weakness. So they become 'strong' by bottling up their woes and keeping mum until depression finally becomes their end. My dear black woman, I do not want this to be your lot. I need you to know that getting help is not a weakness in any form. Yes, it takes a lot of courage to open up to anyone about their problem. What if they judge me? What if they don't understand me? What if I'm going crazy? These and many more are the questions that pop up in your heart from time to time. It is perfectly normal to have these fears. But don't let them dictate your life. You are in charge of your life; act like it. There's one great line in 'Summer Day,' a poem by Mary Oliver which reads, 'So, what is it you want to do with your one wild and precious life?'

I am asking you this question too. What do you want to do with your one wild and precious life? Are you going to spend it depressed? I hope you do not want to spend your life in depression.

Until you open up, you'd not realize that there are thousands and millions of people battling depression too. You are not alone. Depression makes you feel like you're the only one in this life. Like nobody loves you nor cares about you. That's one great lie that you should never believe. You are greatly loved and cherished. Your friends and loved ones do not love to see you wallowing in depression. I have learned that people with depression are perfect at masking it and acting like everything is normal. You wonder how I know this, right? I've had my bouts of depression in the past. I've once lost every will to live too. I am glad I did not let go of life. During that time of my life, I locked everyone out and cried about how it was just me. I find it funny and ironic now. Depression made me lock people out and still lament how alone I was. Sad stuff. People only see what you show them. Most of my folks didn't even realize I was depressed because I hid it so well. You know, people do not have eyes that can bore through your brain to see what goes on there. I beg of you, my dear black woman, to speak up.

You could talk to your family members or trusted friends. What if you do not understand people around you who would listen to you talk about your depression?

Speak to a professional. No one can help you deal with your depression better than a therapist. Some people shy away from speaking to a therapist about their depression because they fear being ridiculed or judged. Most of these fears exist only in your head. Do you know why I hold this belief? Therapists are adept at helping you deal with your mental health problems.

They'd understand you more than you can ever imagine.

When I was diagnosed with clinical depression years ago, my doctor had recommended that I see a therapist. I didn't buy the idea at all. I couldn't even stand the thought of opening up to anyone about my demons. I stayed by myself, self-destructing and fading away. I later saw the need for a therapist when my condition became severe. My therapist was excellent. I owe a lot of my healing to him. My dear, I am not dismissing the possibility of encountering a lousy therapist. It happens. But don't allow the prospect of that to keep you from the healing you need. Go to the therapist with an open mind. If it doesn't work, go to another one. To avoid the stress that comes with going from therapist to therapist, you could have a doctor recommend one for you. Doctors seem to know the best therapists for different kinds of people.

There's one mistake that people make when getting help for depression. People would rather talk to their friends or people who are not in the best positions to help them. Your friend could be kind and understanding, but that doesn't make your friend a therapist. Remember this as often as you can. You know, a good player won't always make a great coach. It is like this with therapy too. Every reasonable person isn't a therapist.

So, my dear woman, I urge you never to be ashamed to reach out for help when depression knocks at your door. You are greatly loved and unique, and you have everything you need to heal from your depression.

Key Points

There is nothing shameful about depression; I beg you to remember this always. People may not always see that you're depressed if you do not say it. Don't be afraid nor ashamed. Get help. I believe that you'll heal. I know you will.

1. It is not your fault that you are depressed. Please do not feel bad about it.

2. You have all you need to heal from depression.

3. Depression is not a death sentence.

4. Over 80% of people who suffer from depression heal eventually. You, too, will heal.

Recovering From Depression Is a Gradual Process

The fastest way to get caught up in your depression is by setting a timer for your healing. 'I must be healed completely by the end of January.' You know, I've met people like this who love to fix specific time frames for their healings. It's one excellent idea, but it never works like that. Hurrying through recovery will only end in hurting just you.

You must understand that healing is a gradual process on your healing journey, especially when it involves mental health issues. You know one thing I've learned about this mental health thing? I've learned that mental illnesses always take longer to heal than physical conditions or injuries. Diseases are easiest to treat when they have a name. For instance, a person gets bitten by a snake. The snake slithers away swiftly after the bite. The victim goes to the doctor. The doctor would need some time to find out the exact time of the snake bite. Of course, treatment would commence immediately to save the victim's life. But, most of the treatments given to the victim would be wild guesses until the exact snake is known.

It is not like this with physical illnesses because of the ease of identifying the condition.

There would be times you would get frustrated working on healing. You might even desire to give up and continue living with depression. But that is the point where you need to fight the most. No, not fistfights and hair-pulling. This type requires you to not give up on your healing, no matter how distant it might seem. Also, never let other people's experience with recovery make your own experience into a lot of frustration.

Some people heal faster than others. Some heal very slowly as well. Sometimes, you may feel incapable of healing because of the incredible amount of time you put into it. You could even become more depressed by trying to heal as other people do.

For this reason, I always advise black women to heal by themselves. Begin by studying and understanding your healing process. If you know it fully, you'll stop trying to heal like another person. My dear black woman, heal the way you desire to. Take your time. But while at it, do not introduce toxicity into it. Do you get what I mean? I'll talk about it more in the next section.

Key Points

Many people give up on overcoming depression because they feel incapable of healing. Every one of us can heal from depression. But not all of us understand our healing processes. Understanding your healing process will keep you safe from a lot of troubles. Find the critical points for this section below.

1. Healing takes time; it is not magic.

2. Study and understand your healing process. It'll help you manage your emotions and deal with your depression better.

3. Do not allow any space for toxicity in your healing process.
4. Different people heal differently. Don't make anyone's healing process your process. You'll end up frustrated.

Incorporating Toxicity In Your Healing Process

Does this topic sound strange to you? Well, it doesn't seem to me. In a bid to heal from trauma as quickly as possible, people sometimes incorporate toxicity into their healing processes. Is it still confusing now? I'll explain it more lucidly.

So, a girl is depressed. She doesn't want to come to terms with that she's depressed and needs help. She tries to get past it all by herself. She tries to elicit some catharsis by listening to depressing music and reading sad books. She does this intending to overwhelm herself with her depression. You know, when we feel emotions like depression very violently, we might 'cry' it out. And that could help with healing. You wonder how I know this. Don't you? Well, I used to incorporate toxicity a lot into my healing processes. She is getting a new partner just after the previous one ended things with me in a bid to make the previous one jealous and angry. I find it hilarious and stupid now because I'm the one that gets hurt in the end.

Incorporating toxicity into your healing process is one of the most harmful things you could ever do to yourself. The truth is, a few people do it and come out fine. Many others don't. They'd only succeed at getting deeper into depression.

Some even become suicidal. No matter how much time your healing takes, I beg you not to become toxic in your quest for healing.

Remember what I told you in the earlier section? Healing is a very gradual process. It doesn't happen all at once. It would be best if you were patient with yourself. It would help if you were kind to yourself.

Sometimes, you might begin to incorporate toxicity into your healing process without knowing it. You'd only notice after a considerable amount happens. I know a good way to avoid this. You could start with journaling everything you do concerning your healing. Then you go back to check them at calculated intervals. Doing this can help you retrace any wrong steps early enough. You could also try speaking with a confidant from time to time about all the things that your healing makes you do. I prefer the first method. I feel like myself the most when I use it.

Key Points

In your quest for healing, you have to be deliberate and careful not to incorporate toxic processes into your recovery. Find the critical points for this section below.

1. Toxicity and healing are like fire and water; they do not mix.
2. Be intentional about your recovery.
3. Journaling your healing process can help you retrace wrong steps quickly.
4. Be patient with yourself.

Healing Begins The Moment You Say Yes To It

I've been going on and on about healing. So, I'm dedicating the whole of this section to answering the question. How does healing come? It is a straightforward answer. Healing begins the very moment you say yes to it. Sometimes, I see healing as a groom proposing to a bride. You know the part where the groom asks will you marry me right? That's what healing does too. In this case, you are the bride. Healing is the groom. No matter how deep you are, the very moment you say yes to healing, it will begin to disappear bit by bit like the moon disappears at the onset of the morning.

A lot of things in life come with choices and choosing. But depression is not one of those things, though. It doesn't take permission from you before it visits as it comes like an unexpected period. And you'd have to deal with it until you gather enough strength to eliminate it. I know you got curious here. Like, is it possible to eliminate depression? Yes, my love. It is very much possible. People have been getting over depression since a long time ago, and that won't change at all. Some people argue that depression doesn't go away. They say it hides inside a person and comes out when triggered. Before I go on, I will leave you with a few sentences about depression triggers for better understanding. Your triggers are simply those things that make you depressed. They trigger you. Different things trigger different people. Depression triggers in another person. Aye, people are differently wired even in something like this.

Now, I have been able to establish the fact that depression is very much curable. If you are among the misinformed people who hold a contrary belief, the hour of your unlearning has come. I understand that with certain levels of depression, healing might seem like an impossible thing. But be constantly reminded that it is not. Are you confused? Don't you know how to go about this healing thing anymore? Do you feel like you'll be depressed all your life? I've felt these feelings too. You are not alone at all.

Believe me. Start your recovery from depression by saying yes to healing. Deciding to heal from depression is one of those decisions no one can make for you but yourself. So, woman up and say yes to recovery. You'll be amazed at how much progress you'll make.

Key Points

A lot of things change when you make a decision. You begin to heal from depression when you make that one decision to heal. I urge you to make that one decision today, my dear black woman. Will you?

1. Your healing begins the very moment you decide to heal.

2. You have all it takes to recover from depression.

3. Depression is very much curable.

4. No matter how deep you are in depression, it all begins to change when you decide.

Support Groups; You Are Not Alone

These days, there are a lot of support groups available for people who once battled depression and those who still fight it. Fighting depression is exhausting. Depression makes you feel like you're all by yourself, right? Like you are that one unlucky person. It is all a lie. First, you're not alone. Second, you're not unlucky.

Joining a support group for depression is an effective way to deal with it. Somehow, support groups have a way of reminding you that you're not alone over and over again. Instead of recoiling into your shell and trying to fight by yourself, how about joining a support group? It isn't easy at all, I know. But it is worth it. Sometimes, the things you'd find about depression online are not applicable in real life. Nothing comes close to meeting with people who have wined and dined with depression. With them, you'd always find a reason to keep on living. To keep on fighting. They have an excellent way of motivating you to keep up with your antidepressants and therapies.

Also, people who suffer from depression find it very challenging to build and sustain relationships the way other people do. Support groups will help you break through that barrier. Do you know why? You'd have to socialize with people there. You'll hear people share their depression stories and how they overcame it. You'll hear people talk about their relapses. You'll hear people talk about therapists that they do not like and laugh at. At some point, you'll share your own stories too.

Joining a support group is not a weakness, my love. It would help if you mustered the courage to try it. I hope you get to join the perfect support group for you, I hope you like it there, and I also hope you fight depression and win. I know that you will win. Do you not remember that you come from a generation of women who wear strength and survival-like crowns?

Key Points

At first, a support group might seem like a bad idea to you. But believe me when I say it is not. It embodies a lot of good things that you'd certainly love to explore. Find the critical points for this section below.

1. Support groups can help you fight your depression better.
2. You are not alone.
3. It would be best if you had as much support as you could get.
4. Support groups can help you make your social skills better.

My dear black woman, we have come to the end of this chapter. If you noticed, this chapter is way

longer than the other ones. It is a deliberate
action. I put a lot of attention and soul into
writing this chapter just for you. You know,
depression is the number one mental illness that
black women face. It is only fitting that I do
enough justice to it. I hope this chapter helps
you greatly as you fight depression.

The next chapter will be all about body
positivity; let's explore! I've got so much in store
for you.

Chapter Nine

*I can't think of any better representation of beauty
than someone unafraid to be herself.*
—Emma Stone.

Body Positivity and The Black Woman

Do not think about cute photographs and social media posts when I talk about body positivity. Instead, look inside you and answer this one question. Do you genuinely love and accept your body? I need you to be honest with me here, my dear black woman. But most importantly, be open to yourself. Everyone seems to know a lot about body positivity. But the irony of the whole thing is this; people get body shamed more now than ever. What do we know about the #bodypositivity, which has become very dominant in our everyday language?

What does body positivity mean? It simply refers to the social movement that focuses on the total acceptance of all body types, gender, skin tone, abilities, etc. The keywords that you should note here are 'total acceptance.' With body positivity, there are no exclusions. It is common knowledge that many black women get bullied in various ways because they are black women. It sounds crazy. But it is the truth. Black women get maltreatment for daring to be so rich in melanin.

For daring to own a forest of afro on their heads. For simply being black. I used to wonder why black women get bullied for being themselves. It took me quite a while to know that people try to destroy what they envy or can't be.

Every day, the media is agog with body positivity pros. But it isn't precisely so in real life. No, I'm not saying everyone that preaches the gospel of body positivity in the media is fake. I'm simply making you realize that not everyone that talks about body positivity practices it. Some of them do it to go with the crowd. Some do it to get favors, even. But don't you ever let them discourage you from wearing your body with pride as you should. Tell me, if you do not carry yourself with dignity, who will do it for you? Nobody. A good number of black women are yet to know this. People give your body the same treatment you give to it. If you carry your body like a piece of shit, trust people to double the energy for you. But I believe that that's not what you want for yourself. So, carry your body with pride and treat it like a queen. You'd see that people would treat your body as such too. The most beautiful women can master the singular art of carrying themselves well.

I love my body so much that I can't help taking gorgeous photographs of myself all the time to admire all the beauty in me. I don't remember exactly how I began to love my body the way I do now. I do not even have a single memory of me hating my body and wishing to change a thing about me. I love my face with the hormonal acne that comes at intervals. I love my thighs with stretch marks on them. When I hear people say they detest stretch marks, it makes me wonder. How could anyone not love such gorgeous stripes? But then, I understand that taste differs. What I would kill for could irritate you. You know, beauty is relative. It comes in different forms and styles. Everyone mustn't fit into your idea of beauty. People should be free to be beautiful like themselves. Yes, I am beautiful like myself. You are beautiful like you. Isn't that fascinating?

My parents played a significant role in making me love my body right from childhood. They gave me the best compliments. They gave me the freedom to wear my body with as much pride as I wanted. I grew up thinking I was a princess. But I didn't live in a castle or have many maids like the Disney princesses. I was my parents' princess. My parents never failed to remind me that I was the most beautiful child they had ever seen. Their words always got into my head. I'd stand before my bedroom mirror and smile at myself. My mother said. I grinned like an angel. Thinking of it now, I wonder how my mother got to know how angels smile.

I understand that not everyone grew up in a loving home and had a beautiful childhood as I did. Body positivity might be a challenging thing for such people. But it is not impossible, and that's the good thing. That's one wonderful thing I love in this life. I love how things begin to change when we make up our minds about things. Body positivity begins to take meaning in your own life the moment you permit it to do so. Of course, you'd encounter people and things that would make you feel like you're not enough. The most beautiful people meet them too. Do not pay them a mind. Your opinion about you is superior to anyone else's. When I do something that makes me happy, and someone else tries to ruin it, I remind myself boldly that my opinion is the most important. Nothing else matters.

Body positivity is not a one-time thing. You know that don't get positive today and become negative tomorrow. It doesn't work like that because you'd have to pick a stand. I'd advise you to choose body positivity, though. Nothing compares to its excellence!

Suppose you're used to not being a body positivity kind of woman; switching all of a sudden would most likely be very difficult for you. That is why I advise you to take it little by little—one step at a time. The first step you should begin with is self-acceptance. You'll read more of it in the next section of this chapter.

Key Points

Different people see body positivity through different lenses. For some, it's just one of those things people say. For others, it is the very core of existence. Body positivity is one of the best things that has ever happened to humanity. Yes, that's how I see it! Find the critical points for this section below.

1. The first step you need to take in your body positivity journey is self-acceptance.

2. Body positivity is way beyond social media posts and hashtags. It encompasses the whole beauty of human existence.

3. You are most beautiful when you accept your body with all of its perfections and flaws.

4. People's opinion of your body doesn't matter at all. Could you not treat them like they do?

Self-Acceptance and Body Positivity

I said self-acceptance is the first step to your body positivity journey in the previous section. Without self-acceptance, body positivity wouldn't even exist. If you look deeper, you'll see that people who are genuinely into body positivity are people who have accepted themselves wholly.

What is self-acceptance? In simple words, it is embracing everything that makes you who you are. A lot of things come together to create a person. Some people are lucky enough to have more good experiences than bad experiences. Others are not as lucky. Some people have known more terrible experiences than they have known good ones. That's the way life swings sometimes. For the former, self-acceptance might not be a tricky thing. A good number of them wouldn't even hesitate to share their life stories with you.

Body positivity might seem like a farce for the second group of people who have known more tears than laughter. You know, people do not love to share sorrowful tales about themselves. People like this may have trouble accepting themselves. Some of them have lives that do not make them happy. Asking such people to be optimistic about their bodies and selves, in general, is like asking them to flaunt their traumas.

This set of people would have to do some unlearning. Life becomes much easier when people do not throw away the experiences that shaped them. I once read this book about a fire accident survivor. In the book, the survivor told her story. She said after her wounds healed, she became suicidal. She couldn't just bear to see the scars every day of her life. She also locked everyone out of her life because the spots made her begin to hate herself. Somehow, she got professional help. Her life came alive again when she stopped hiding her scars. She started to call them her trophies. Do you know why she called them trophies? They showed that she wrestled with fire and won. I smile anytime I remember this.

I shared this story with you because it is one beautiful way to look at life. Not only does it help you heal from past hurts, but it also strengthens you. There's no need to beat yourself up and lament every day about the things that have happened to you. Bring out those scars and stop hiding away. It is not great to hide trophies.

Now, I'm back to talking about accepting your body just the way it is. There's one thing that you must know. If all women eat the same food and do the same exercises, they still have different body types. Body types do not arise by just exercise, diets, and waist trainers. It is more than that. Genetics and environmental factors all have their roles to play. I think genetics plays the most prominent role in determining body types. Every other thing comes secondary. Your body cannot be like the one of every girl you admire on the gram. You have your unique body. Your body stands out from the crowd. That body that you loathe so much is someone else's dream body. Crazy, right? But that doesn't stop it from being true. Be proud of your cellulite, your jutting collarbone, your small breasts, your full breasts, your small eyes, your big eyes. Be proud of all your features. You are beautiful in every part. I was hoping you could do something for me right now.

Please go to the mirror closest to you and peer into it. Now, smile at the angel that looks back at you from the mirror. Don't you love what you see? You are the angel in the mirror. How wonderful!

To embrace your body better and love it better, take your time to study it. You know, different body types have different needs. Study your body type and find out what your body needs, From Diet type, wardrobe type, and so on. Doing this will help you greatly in caring for your body and carrying it with pride. You could check out the styles of people whose body types are similar to yours. Trust me; you'll be glad that you did. But, you are under no compulsion to do this. My black women are creative geniuses. I believe in your unique ability to create excellent styles for yourself. Your body is like a flower. The more your nurture it, the prettier it gets. So, my dear woman never quit nurturing that gorgeous body of yours. The world is thousand times more colourful and stunning because your beauty dwells in it. You know this, don't you?

Key Points

1. You are beautiful and perfect just the way you are. It would help if you had no one's validation to stay beautiful too.

2. If all women did the same things simultaneously, they would still have different body types.

3. Your body is perfect and full of beauty.

4. Your scars are trophies. Never be ashamed of them.

5. Self-acceptance is the first step you need to take in your body positivity journey.

What Is The Definition of True Beauty?

A lot of people have tried over and over again to define beauty. But the truth they fail to realize is that beauty has no definition. Why will anyone try to put something as broad and endlessly attractive as beauty in a box by defining it?

A lot of people try to give beauty a label by defining it. It makes me wonder. I wouldn't say I like tags. In the words of the famous poet Walt Whitman, I contain multitudes. Yes, I include too many things to limit myself by labels and definitions. Black women have a lot of excellencies too. Please don't limit yourself by tags and others' intentions who do not even explore beauty in all forms.

Every day, different people come up with varying definitions of beauty. It is the trend now. It has become so common that the moment you ask people about beauty, you'd get almost the same answers from everyone. They'd mention a specific eye category and particular hair color and tell you it is the most beautiful thing in the world. I find the whole thing sad, but it also makes me realize that many would gladly accept that they are not beautiful because they do not meet a certain standard. Well, I do not blame them so much. I blame society. I blame some modelling agencies more. Talking about modelling agencies, I remember something that happened at high school.

It happened to one of my seniors and friend. We called her Maggie. Maggie was passionate about modelling and walking on the biggest runways while rocking the best brands. Her passion for modelling was so beautiful to see. I've never met anyone passionate about modelling the way Maggie was. She put the whole of herself into it. We were overjoyed when Maggie got invited for an interview by one big modelling agency at the time. We were already looking forward to Maggie becoming a star already. We were more than convinced that she would breeze through the interview. I mean, asking Maggie about modelling is asking her about her life. Who would fail to answer questions about their own lives well?

All our joy and enthusiasm died when Maggie told us how the interview went. Of course, she did very well in the question and answer part of the interview. You are curious as to where Maggie failed. She wasn't tall enough. Yes, that was the reason. It hurt me so much to see Maggie crying. The helplessness of the situation made it sadder. It was so unfair. Not like people made themselves or something. If people had the power to create themselves, there would have been a lot of gorgeousness in this life. You know, it would be a competition of beauty, poise, and class.

The thing with most modeling agencies is that they are very unrealistic. If you follow them as closely as I do, you will notice that they seem to follow a particular pattern. Has it ever occurred to you why almost all the top models are slender and tall? That is what they define beauty to be. But I am glad that many agencies have also included different body types in their walks. It makes it all more realistic. I love it when fashion is natural. That's the issue I have with some TV commercials too. You'd see the girls some sanitary pad brands to advertise, and you'd think periods are all sweet and rosy when it's not even anywhere close to that in real life.

My dear black woman, I beg you not to let yourself get so caught up in the stereotypical and crazy definitions of beauty that you begin to lose yourself. Take your time and admire all of your features whenever that starts to happen. Spend time loving those parts that excite you the most. Remind yourself about the graciousness of your body. It's not easy having a perfect body like your own. Carry that body with pride. It's okay if you feel better in your body by enhancing it. Yes, it happens. Don't be sad about feeling this way. A little more ass would make your body as perfect as you want it, right? Small boobs will make you proud of your body. Go for the body that you love. Things you want can happen with consistent workout sessions and better diets. You might need surgery for others too.

Whichever ones you choose, I urge you to get them the right way. Many women die in the course of going through beauty processes the wrong way. I do not want you to add to the numbers. I know you do not want that for yourself too. So, love, take your time and get your dream body the right way.

Remember, your definition of beauty is valid. You do not have to bend to any beauty standard. You are beautiful all by yourself.

Key Points

1. Beauty has no one definition.

2. You are perfect, so is your body.

3. You can get your dream body through workouts and surgeries. Don't let anyone make you feel guilty for going for the kind of body you desire.

Chapter Ten

The Black Woman and Failure

Success is stumbling from failure to failure with no loss of enthusiasm.

--Winston S. Churchill

I'm guessing by the title above that your mind already diverted to an incident or two where you had an objective in mind but couldn't meet it along the line. Or you did, but the outcome wasn't what you desired. Did you sink yourself into the hole of depression and self-loathe? Or did you let yourself feel the emotions that come with failing for a brief moment, and shake it off, saying to yourself that you are strong and you've got all it takes to succeed?

Everyone comes across failure at some point in their lives. Even that big-time reality star you drool about and think their life is a bed of roses has experienced loss. Not once, not twice. The billionaires, social media personalities, your favorite artists, and other thriving characters that you look up to have all experienced to fail. Most have come out to tell tales of their pasts and how they got to the top, while some sit back and act as if everything has always been excellent, whereas it's a sham. My dear black woman, do not allow these to deceive you that you'll begin to access yourself negatively, letting room for anxiety, depression, and even envy.

When we talk about failure, most people say it is one's inability to reach a particular goal or do something that you must or wish to do. Even babies fail. Yes, my black queen. When they try to start walking, only to fall back down, that's failing. And the teenager who's continuously in a battle with his books in preparation for a math test only to end up failing the test. He'd cry out and even go as far as hating that subject. But that is not always the case. Some people take up their failure as a challenge to do better, and I have a personal story to share concerning this.

When I was a teenager, I was conflicted between choosing the sciences or arts many years ago. My parents were very supportive and said they would offer their support no matter my choice. So I decided I was going to study medicine to be a doctor. I had always heard the most impressive and fascinating tales of doctors; how they contributed to the growth and saving of humanity. Take, for instance, Ben Carson, who made the separation of conjoined twins possible. It served as a trigger, and I wanted to badly do something worth being in the Guinness book of records. Despite this, there was a doubt looming within me about my decision.

I wanted to be a thoracic surgeon and make a remarkable impact in the medical world. Still, there was an irony, black Queen, and do you know what it was? I didn't have what it took. You know, becoming a surgeon involves putting your fears asides and going all in, but I do not like to see blood at all. The mere sight of it makes my hair stand on edge. I also knew my academic strengths and weaknesses, and I was more robust in the arts. Still, because I wanted to be a surgeon, I tried to get over the feeling and went as far as taking the exams for the course. Well, you can guess what happened. I failed woefully.

No, I'm not dumb. The thing is, people don't seem to understand the concept of failing. Many think failing at something means you're not good enough. But it was not so for me. I already knew my strengths and had my parents support me in whatever I chose. My mom advised me earlier to go for the art courses, but I was pig-headed. I told her my desire, and she agreed to give it a shot. But with my failure in that shot, I realized one thing. I was forcing things.

Deep down, I knew I would end up in the arts, but I also wanted to have the experience of being a surgeon because of the story I had read about Ben Carson. I failed at it, I agreed that I would be better off in the arts, and it's been a fantastic ride. Of course, I sulked and cried for days; let myself feel the negative emotions that come with failing. But I did not let them consume me. I had to get up and try something better because failure isn't final.

Some people fail and refuse to try something else. They keep on repeating the same thing over and over again. If you know something isn't working for you, there are many alternatives to try out. Indeed, something out there must interest you. You'll find that one thing that'd set your heart on fire if you look deeper. That you failed at being an artist doesn't mean you'll fail at being an actor or actress. You have to understand that some things are not just for you. Failing at them is the universe's way of letting you know because the worst that would happen is that the goal may haunt you when you eventually achieve it. Yes, my beautiful black queen, it happens. Many people today would have been living their lives in the most peaceful ways on earth. But they were so focused on getting something that they failed at repeatedly; they delved into illegal things, which eventually devoured them.

Key Points

Many people have had more than one experience of what it is to fail. Some see it as a prerequisite to a truly successful life; others believe you don't have to die to be successful. Whatever you choose to think, I want you to understand that failure isn't a death sentence but a step to self-realization. The critical points for this section are below:

1. It's okay to fail; no one should judge you for failing.

2. If you fail, you can always try again, or
    it's the universe's way of telling you, "this
    isn't it."

3. Experiencing failure exposes you to your
    strengths and weaknesses and helps your
    personal growth.

4. It's okay to feel the negative emotions of
    failing, but you shouldn't let it define you.

Redefining The Concept of Failure

Earlier, I stated that most people believe failure entails not reaching their desired goals. But it is more than that. Failure is a thing of the mind, like when you do well in a test, scoring as high as 80% in your grades. Still, you consider your performance a failure because you set your mind to 90%. Let's go deeper.

Do you know that some people look up to you, and even the smallest of your actions is a big deal to them, and they're like, "Wow, this lady is amazing!" Yes, my beautiful black woman, some people think you're doing just right, that when you tell them you got a job with good pay, instead of the one you wished for, they'll laugh and walk you through how far you've come. A promotion from a measly paying job to a better one, which, however, isn't what you desire, is not failure. The thing is, we become so focused on the wrong side and choose to forget that there were even good times. Writing this makes me emotional as I remember an incident some years back. I want to share it with you because I want you to understand what I'm saying entirely.

Everyone says you shouldn't focus too much on the wrong side but on how far you've come, and it took me quite a while to realize this; to truly understand and abide by it.

I used to be the type of person who gets anxious and irritable whenever I'm low on cash, and it happened to be a big issue for me. During such times, I would take out my anger and frustration on my family and friends, setting me apart from most of them. I pushed them away. I considered myself a failure to achieve what I had planned to until a particular day. One of my friends told me some things that I still remember vividly. He asked me to check my pictures from the previous year and what I noticed. The first thing I noticed was my phone. I was no longer using the phone I used the last year because I had bought a better one without even selling the previous one.

I also noticed I had gained a few pounds and many other things I would not want to bore you with by listing. The summary is that the comparison I made of myself in the previous year and myself the following year was an eye-opener. It showed me that my inability to achieve some goals did not mean I was a failure. You don't have to pressure yourself so much that you refuse to believe there's any progress in your life. Take the saying of Oprah Winfrey that "If you look at what you have in life, you'll always have more. If you look at what you don't have in life, you'll never have enough," and put it to heart.

In our quest to redefine failure, I'll discuss what can help you understand the concept of failure and see it as more than your inability to attain that desired goal. The first is being a novice at something.

When you're new to something, there's every tendency that you won't get it right the first time. I mean, how can you be perfect at what you just started? Perfection is all about flawlessness, the highest degree of skill. You can't just wake up one morning and do something you've not done flawlessly. It's not magic. The baby who just began toddling is bound to fall a few dozen times, or the cyclist who has no initial experience of cycling will have a few scratches from falling. It's always like that. So why beat yourself up for something you just started doing? Yes, it's been months; you're a fast learner, so why is it taking so much time? I know. All these questions are pricking hard at your mind, and all you do all day is sigh and shake your head in weariness. Listen to me, my beautiful black queen; you don't need any of that unnecessary stress and overthinking. Everything will move at its own pace. Access yourself, where you were before you started and where you are now, and you'll see that you're making some progress. But if you think you're not, then it's a hint that you're not doing a few things, or you're not doing things the right way.

Another thing to note and ask yourself is if you're a perfectionist. I can not outrightly say that being a perfectionist is a bad thing. I do not believe that it is terrible because it has its perks. However, I'm not too fond of the excessive stress that comes with it. In trying to attain perfection, you're faced with constant anxiety and worry about if you're doing or looking alright. You say inwardly to yourself, "I have to get this right without a flaw," and ask yourself specific questions as a result of self-doubt like, "am I still on course?" and the "what ifs?"

Being a perfectionist is working hard to put things in order, even if it takes your time and energy, and you wouldn't mind finishing late. I have a perfectionist friend, and I can say most times that people are the way they are because of their upbringing. Some people are so scared of experiencing failure because the society where they grew up shamed loss and extolled success. They made loss seem taboo, which is more impactful on a child when it comes from the parents. Imagine having a parent who scolds you repeatedly when you get a grade less than an A and goes as far as comparing you to your peers who happen to do better. It's disturbing and even more problematic that parents still engage in this act. So you can correctly guess how such a child from these parents would be, endlessly questioning their actions and assessing themselves to do better, at times being reclusive or unhappy.

A perfectionist does not like to align with failure, and that's the issue here. They believe that since they are putting in much more effort than their peers, the outcome should indeed be better, and when life does its thing with bias, they get into a hell hole of depression. If you are a perfectionist, you should relate. You have incredibly high standards, and sometimes you're scared that they're too high, and you end up procrastinating because you're afraid of failure. No, my beautiful black queen, you have to understand that failure is a part of life and helps you grow. Rather than beat yourself up when you know you tried your absolute best, why not focus on what was missing instead of sulking all day and telling yourself that you're not enough.

I used to criticize my perfectionist friend a lot, and we would even fall out occasionally because, let's say, we didn't align well at that time. I was the carefree type, and she was the ever anxious one. She was always so bothered about me, and I watched her laugh over how worried she could be. You only live once. I would always say, so don't be afraid to do what you've intended to do. If you're a perfectionist and the opposing sides are eating you up, you have to seek help and also try to tone it down a little. Believe in yourself, try your best, and take solace in the fact that you put in your all. If it still doesn't work out, you have to get up and try again.

In redefining failure, you might agree that it's not about not being able to achieve a goal, so you've decided to try, but you still end up failing.

Then, it could be that there's a systemic bias against you, my black woman. In a situation where you put your all to work assigned to you, it's even clear to everyone in the company that you're doing great. Still, a high-ranking officer comes at you and talks down on your work because of their bias against your color. My beautiful black woman, I do not wish you to beat yourself up because someone is prejudiced against you. You don't have to go on with the sleepless nights in an attempt to "satisfy" such people because the truth is that they'll never be satisfied.

If you cannot leave them, you'll have to think of ways to work with them. Arm yourself with all the qualities we've discussed. Have the courage to speak your mind in the face of oppression, and if you're able to do this, you won't have to feel you're failing when really, you aren't.

Key Points

Many people believe failure is all about being unable to attain your desired goal, but I think it goes past this. Sometimes, things are hindering your progress that you fail to check, so failure reminds you to take note and sets you on the right course, that is, if you let it, of course. Let's go through the points in this section:

1. That you didn't achieve your aim doesn't mean you failed. You need to stop and assess yourself.

2. Think of what's missing or why you think you failed, and try again.

3. If you're a novice at something, you cannot achieve perfection immediately in redefining failure. You'll fall at certain times. But, rise!

4. Sometimes, failure isn't your fault, so you shouldn't be too hard on yourself.

5. You could be doing great, but someone biased towards you would always fail to acknowledge it. Don't let that define your progress.

Starting Again After a Failure

No one likes to fail, and successful people dread failure even more because they've tasted success and failing is barely an option to them. Have you ever watched your house burn down from scratch? I have, and that very day broke me to pieces. It was shattering because I built the house with my sweat, time, and money, sustained a couple of injuries and went broke a few hundred times to make sure the house got finished. Only to watch it get razed to the ground by a raging fire and unable to do anything tangible. I sulked for weeks and barely gave myself any attention because one of my fears happened. One day, I stumbled across the story of J.K Rowling, Harry Potter's author, on the net. Rowling's story was that she was a single mom living off welfare and suicidal when she had the idea of the story on her way from Manchester to London on a train. Rowling's original pitch for the Harry Potter series was called the bluff by the first twelve places she sent it to, but she persisted. Today, she has about 400 million books sold, and it all hit deeply. Then, I was at my lowest, so I understood what it was to fail, and at the same time, I knew what it was to succeed. I made up my mind; I had to start again.

The first thing I did in starting again was to accept responsibility for my failure. I know I said sometimes you're not the one at fault, and that's fine. But when you're confident you are, like I was, you have to set your ego aside and own up to your actions. How was I at fault that my house was razed to the ground by fire? Good question you might have. To finish the construction, I cut corners and used substandard materials for the roofing and wiring. The day it caught fire, it rained cats and dogs, and I was away at work. In summary, before anyone could do anything, the fire had already grown too big.

At first, I was reluctant to accept that I was at fault. I blamed the companies that manufactured the materials; I inwardly blamed my neighbors, who I assumed didn't want to do anything about the fire. Still, with time, I realized it was entirely my fault. I didn't go for quality building materials. And blaming my neighbors for my misfortune was altogether unfair and immature because they weren't at the scene on time, neither were they trained firefighters. Suppose there's something you failed at, maybe a project work or did not get a promotion as you anticipated. In that case, the first thing you have to do is check yourself and if you're at fault, be humble enough to accept it.

The next step to starting again is to pick up the pieces of your life again. My strong black woman, hurting doesn't make you weak, you're allowed to sulk all day and sob over that failure, but as I've always said, when you finish, you have to get up and keep going. You can always set things right. If there are people that say bad things about you, trust that there'll also be good people to repair that image, but you must first apologize if you're in the wrong. Or did you get kicked out of work? There are always different opportunities out there for you. Explore all of them.

The third step is to remind yourself of your past successes constantly. Did you bag that degree? That's a success. Did you graduate from college? It's a success. Got a job? Got married? Started something you always wanted to? Attended an occasion you had always wished to attend? They're all successes. Success doesn't have to be significant. That workout you completed is a success. Whatever you constantly desire to do is your success. When you're feeling down because you failed, take out a pen and write out ten things you did successfully. You'll see that there's even more. Don't think you're worthless just because of a failure. No black queen, you are a conqueror, and you have all it takes to succeed. If this isn't your first time failing, take a quick look back at your past failures and successes. Everyone makes mistakes that can lead to losses, but just as you recover from that previous failure, comfort yourself with the belief that you'll also recover from your present failure. It will make the process faster for you and spur you to your next step - making a decision.

When you finish thinking deeply about your mistake or failure, accepting your faults, and reminding yourself of your successes, make a decision. And I do not mean that you do nothing, for it is in itself a decision. But it is a negative one capable of impeding your progress and, worse still, causing damage to your life. You know what you want, beautiful black woman, and it is only proper that you decide to get it. If it requires you to take a course on it, reading intensively, communicating with people around, and seeking advice from those knowledgeable in that field, do it. You're on a self-development journey, and failure is part of it. What is the reason you failed? Can you try again on your own? If not, then you need to decide to talk to someone, probably a therapist, friend, or confidant.

Now you're done deciding, the final step is to forget about your past and focus on your vision. It may seem hard, but thinking about it would only make it harder. It's your past, and you can't change your history, can you? So why bother so much, queen? You have only the present guaranteed, and the best you can do is make good use of it. If you're going to continue on that journey, do it. If you wish to start something else, by all means, begin.

Key Points

Failure should teach us, not overcome us. It's not a death sentence but an eye-opener. It should show you what you were doing wrong, not make you feel worthless. You're in charge of what failure can make you think, and let it spur you on to the next success story, my black woman. Here are the key points:

1. No one likes to fail, but they tend to forget that failure is part of what you must experience to succeed.

2. Accepting responsibility for your mistakes is a crucial step to overcoming failure.

3. Rather than soak yourself up in your loss, you should make a list of all your achievements and go over them.

4. You're not worthless because of a mistake. Everyone makes mistakes.

5. Talking to someone would aid your recovery from failure a lot faster, as well as taking that course you always wanted.

We've finally come to the end of this chapter, my dear black woman! It's been an incredible ride with you all the way, and I'm excited to talk to you about what's in the next chapter. Let's go!

Chapter Eleven

On Pedestals and Living For Other People

When you become famous, people can have a powerful yet illusory idea of who you are. You want to live your life, but still, you don't want to let anyone down. I know Ed Vedder, Kurt Cobain, Jerry Cantrell, all those guys felt it. They're smart, real, and all of a sudden, they're put on a pedestal.

---Ann Wilson

Before we begin fully into this chapter, let's clear the air about what it means to be put on a pedestal. When I say someone placed me on a pedestal, it simply means someone thinks of me as a perfect person with no flaws at all. Quite funny, but that is the case where followers or fans put celebrities on pedestals, even when they didn't ask for it, expecting only a particular type of behavior from them. Lovers also put each other on pedestals, with one of them usually the male putting the female on a pedestal. Or it could be anyone; anyone with some distinct feature can be placed on a pedestal by another.

I don't know if you get the point already, my dear black woman. I always laugh whenever I encounter this phrase because I've been in that situation and put someone on a pedestal. Yes, I have first-hand experience with this topic, at least on the relationship level. The one based on popularity is a story about my friend. Don't worry; I'll try to share it all.

Do you remember what we discussed about self-worth in chapter seven? How do some people let others push them around because they believe they're better than themselves and that they're not good enough? That's usually the case when we talk about putting others on pedestals. My black woman, like it or not, you may have or might come across someone or people who would place you on a pedestal, and I want you to get ready for it. It often takes a whole lot from an individual. It narrows your life to only the line the person wants you to thread with them, forgetting that you have a life to live; I hope you understand?

I dated one person who had placed me on a pedestal, and he had himself living for me. The thing is, I didn't intend to make him live only for me, but something just happened, and before I could blink, he was already exhibiting the signs. My ex never faulted me because he admired me so much; he firmly believed I was incapable of doing any wrong. However, with my experiences, I can say that's possible - being obsessed about someone so much that you choose to forget the red flags and live in an illusion. I would have him try to talk things with me regarding a particular negative behavior I could put up with all week, but he'd never be straightforward. I'd make it clear to him that I needed him to speak up, but he just couldn't.

He had placed me above himself from the onset, and although he wanted to communicate with me, he couldn't. I mean, how can you relate well with someone on a higher level than you? That's the idea. I didn't even ask to be there, just like how the person I put on a pedestal did not ask for it. I think, by all means, it is unhealthy to be the one on the pedestal and the one doing the pedestal-placing. No one sees it as a fun thing to be perceived as a god or robot. Sure, it's an ego-booster, but this is by someone constantly looking up to you as a perfect human incapable of errors. It's a big shock to them when you eventually fall short of their expectations. Haha. It's funny because I've been through it even though it was not a fun ride then. When someone places you on a pedestal, as my ex did, they have many questions about their self-worth popping up in their head. Questions like, "how is it you have your life together, and they do not?" or statements like, "everything you are, they're not," and "everyone loves you but not them."

It is not envy per se. Suppose you look at it from a different angle. In that case, it's just a conscious or an intense unconscious admiration that grows into low self-esteem. You know, dear queen, social media is a crazy place. You have people portraying all kinds of genuine and fake lifestyles that you barely know, whether real or not. When you focus entirely on someone more successful than you are, it leaves room for self-doubt and anxiety, and that's no way one should live.

I have a friend called Brandon. He's into music, specifically the electronic dance genre. Brandon once told me that he did not wish to go into hip hop because, to him, it didn't allow you much freedom of getting your privacy, so he stuck to EDM. But even with that, Brandon was perceived by his social media fans as collected, intelligent, and gentlemanly. He wasn't far from what they saw him be, but the truth was that the fans didn't care to know what his interests were or what he indeed was. All they saw was a peaceful, contented artist worth emulating.

One day, Brandon came crying to me that he was in a sex scandal plotted by his foe. Brandon explained he had been going through a lot and was drinking all night in a bar when two girls approached him and led him on. With all evidence against him, most of his so-called fans revolted and called him all sorts of debasing names that left him dazed. That's what being there feels like; You face constant pressure from people who want you to live up to the hype. If you're a popular personality like my friend and perhaps a perfectionist, you'll find yourself striving towards it. Most perfectionists don't like to disappoint their loved ones, so when they realize these loved ones are looking up to them, they try everything to live up to the hype and not hurt them, but most times, it doesn't end well. For some people, they do not want to be on a pedestal, and while the feeling may be nice for a while, in the end, they'll ask you for some form of closure; that is for you to know their truth and understand them. Others are entirely okay with it. Which are you, my dear black woman?

Key Points

While being admired dramatically by someone may feel good, it can pose a problem when they begin to idolize you and expect nothing less from you. These people sometimes forget that you're human too and make mistakes. However, it's up to you, dear black woman, to decide if you want to be on a pedestal or not. The key points are listed below:

1. It's okay to admire someone, but it can become a problem when it gets too much.

2. It would help if you stopped allowing someone to make you doubt your self-worth is an unhealthy practice.

3. If you can't cope with being on a pedestal, you're going to have to let them know eventually.

4. Don't try to be what you aren't to live up to the hype. Being you is the best form of self-care.

5. Before you consciously place someone on a pedestal, ask yourself if you're going to be comfortable if it were you.

Dangers of Being Placed On a Pedestal

There are many side effects of being placed on a pedestal that you might want to avoid at all costs. For emphasis, if you can handle the pressure, no one's stopping you, but otherwise, you have to get out. I don't advise that you allow someone to limit your life by putting you on a pedestal because then you're living the life they're not courageous to live. Remember, I talked about low self-esteem as one factor that leads people to pedestal-placing. For one to rank you above themselves, it means they've concluded that you're better than them and are now watching you achieve a whole chunk of what they wish to. They expect a lot from you, and allowing yourself to this pressure means you are allowing them to tell you how to live your life.

I've seen a lot of mothers place their kids on pedestals. Things they could not achieve as kids tend to impose on the little ones and try to pattern their lives in a certain way favorable to them, but usually not the child. Dear black woman, I need you to veer away from this course and treat your children with all the love they deserve, not idolize them or force them into things they do not like. Even in your marital or relationship life, placing your partner way above you because you feel they're doing you a favor by loving you is wrong. You deserve all the love you can get, and no one should make you feel less, not even yourself. He brought you from grass to grace, that's wonderful and very kind, but it should never be a reason for you to worship him or feel inferior, dear black woman. I do hope you're getting what I'm trying to nail. The essence of this is that it will help your relationship better. With that pedestal out of the way, you can be able to effectively communicate with your partner or child, get to know them, and improve your relationship with them.

Allowing people to put you on a pedestal can ultimately damage you if you're not careful, my beautiful black woman. As I said earlier, you shouldn't dictate what that child should be because it's what you've always wished for, and so also should you not allow anyone to dictate who you are. It's you we're talking about here, no one else but you, and that's all you've got. So you have to take care of yourself and carry yourself with pride. When I was put on a pedestal by my ex, we seemed happy because he didn't want to fault me. You know, he always let me call the shots, and we even rushed into a significant relationship milestone under five months of dating. Everything was all sunshine and roses, but he was dying on the inside. He struggled to know me, but it was all in vain because he had set me up high above him, like going up ahead and putting banana peels on your way. That was what it felt like, and in the end, he blamed me. While my other ex, whom I placed on a pedestal, had me question my abilities as he walked all over me, and the crazy thing was, I let him. He made plans that often didn't involve me, and when I realized, I'd feel like my world had come crashing because, at the time, I was very dependent on him. It's a relationship that stirs negative feelings anytime I remember it, to show the extent of the damage this could cause.

Being placed on a pedestal to the extent that you're living someone else's life has to be the worst kind of punishment to yourself. It fills you with irritation and envy when you see others living their desired lives. You're not; you can't find happiness at your workplace or whatever your pedestal placers want you to do. You're sad or infuriated by someone else's enthusiasm because you don't feel the same way about it pedestal. The only things that inspire you are your reputation, money, and the people's praise, and you sit back and watch life pass you by without actually living. It's sad in the least to say, even more, shameful if you allow it for fame and money.

But again, I repeat, if you enjoy being put on a pedestal and can handle the pressure, by all means, have it your way. But if you don't, you must agree with me that it's detrimental to your growth when you let a partner or society at large dictate how you should live your life.

It's heartbreaking seeing people in their workplace moving about with their minds far away because they do not wish to be there. It's not encouraging to see someone being downtrodden by their partner, and they do nothing because they've placed their partner above them. This section has briefly highlighted the dangers of being placed on a pedestal. The key points are listed thus:

1. You allow people to live your life for you when they deliberately impose their wishes on you.

2. Placing people on pedestals because they've been generous to you isn't the right thing to do.

3. It would help if you didn't dictate another person's life.

4. You're all you've got, so you shouldn't let someone damage you.

5. It's not proper to live someone else's life, especially for fame or money.

How To Stop Living for Other People

My dear black woman, we've come this far in identifying what being on a pedestal and living for other people are about, as well as the dangers attached. I do hope you've accessed yourself if you'd like to be on a pedestal or not. This section is for those who wouldn't want to and how to stop living for other people. There are many ways to stop being placed on a pedestal and living for other people. Also, I'll share tips on how to stop putting people on pedestals. It's going to be a general discussion.

Defining your relationship is crucial to avoid being placed on a pedestal. When you let your partner know that they should see and treat you equally, there'll be less room for assumptions, and they will act accordingly. If I say, "Alright, here are my conditions. I don't want anyone see me as a god; I want us to be able to communicate effectively," she would understand that I don't want to be on a pedestal and act accordingly. You can also apply this method with your fans. Let your fans repeatedly know that you're human, and they shouldn't have high expectations from you more than they should from themselves. People tend to do that a lot, and it's not cool; telling people how to handle their life when they've not even attempted to run theirs. So communicating and laying boundaries is a significant step and being open to your partner about your insecurities.

If you're currently living someone else's life, there's a high chance that you're unhappy, and if that's your case, my beautiful black woman, you need to act. It might be not very easy, I do not know, but you really shouldn't let go of life without at least achieving most of your goals. You have the right to do whatever makes you happy, and every other thing should be next. Let the words of Steve Jobs guide you; "Your time is limited, so don't waste it living someone else's life. Don't be trapped by dogma — living with the results of other people's thinking. Don't let the noise of others' opinions drown out your inner voice. And most importantly, dare to follow your heart and intuition."

If you're used to putting people on pedestals, you also have to stop it. You may think it's hard, but I guarantee it will help you; you'll be on your way to increasing your self-esteem in no time. Firstly, you have to look inside of yourself. Black queen, I'm going to restate this because I need you to understand; there's only you in this game, and you can't afford to lose yourself to others. Are you getting married to that person because he's got all you've always wished for yourself? Why can't you get it? What's stopping you? You have to free yourself and soar high else. You might end up regretting it. Or you're envious of that girl because of her perfect figure? Then focus on it and stay committed to the gym and healthy diets. Most of these things you envy in people require you to be committed to them, so you must imbibe the virtue of commitment.

Key Points

I understand that being placed on a pedestal can be discomforting, so there's no justification for you to put another on it. Work on yourself instead and begin to own your life. The key points are listed below:

1. If you're not comfortable being placed on a pedestal, you must communicate.

2. Achieve most of your goals now that you have the time.

3. Increasing your self-worth and self-love is a significant step to stop putting people on pedestals.

4. Who says you can't be whatever you want to be?

The Ninety Day Plan

Finally, we've come to the last part of this book—the ninety-day plan for managing emotions. I am writing this plan in the simplest way I know how to. I want you to have fun going through the schedule for each day, so I made them very concise and straight to the point. It takes between 21-66 days to build habits, so I am hoping, and I believe that by the time we come to the end of this ninety-day plan, you would have gained a lot of control over your emotions. You'll be needing a notebook to write down certain things. Let's dig in already, shall we?

Week One: Managing Anger

Day One — Breathe In

Some situations cause you to be so angry, and all you want to do is yell at someone or punch someone in the face, but you shouldn't let your anger consume you. Everyone knows that life is not fair, but it is not defined by what happens, instead of by your response to situations. Imagine a situation where someone angers you and retaliates by throwing a punch at the person. You might be unaware of the person's health status, and that one punch could send the person to the other side, with you eventually being sent to jail. So before you take any action in anger, you have to stop, black Queen, and breath in.

Tips for Day One

• Accept that not everyone aligns with you, and some may annoy you.

• Get that life is not a bed of roses and some days are harsh.

• Overall, remind yourself to take a deep breath and think about the consequences of that action you want to take out of anger. You might not like it.

Day Two — Focus On The Bright Side

Now my dear black woman, how did you feel after breathing in again? I imagine you were still angry, but the singular fact that you could stop for a second to live is an outstanding achievement. Some people become so blinded by rage that they completely forget they're supposed to stop taking a deep breath, but remember, this is a journey to control your emotions. I need you to remember always to breathe in, and then you'll be able to see the silver lining. If it's a problem bugging you, you'll be able to stop fussing and eventually find a solution to it and trust me, that's good progress.

Tips for Day Two

•   When you can take a deep breath in, you'll find the light at the end of the tunnel.

•   Remind yourself that it's just a problem, and there's no problem without a solution.

•   Worrying and getting angry have never held positive solutions.

Day Three — Forgive and Let Go

Maybe the breathing technique didn't help in soothing your anger. Can I ask, are you holding a grudge? If yes, the task of this day in particular for you. Holding a grudge is only detrimental to oneself, no matter how you see it. You may wish to punish the person by doing so, but it's a sham. The person may even be unaware of your grudge while you're dying on the inside. Beautiful black woman, let go of that grudge and experience how light your heart can feel without resentment sitting on it. Task yourself today, text that person you've been angry with, ask how they are. It's okay if you don't want to seek closure because of whatever they might have done to you, but forgive them and stop thinking about that hurt because, trust me, it's not worth your stress.

Tips for Day Three

- Holding a grudge only weighs your heart down and affects your happiness.

- Decide to forgive that person today. You'll feel a lot better.

- It's okay if you can't forget the hurt they caused, but you have to forgive and move on.

Day Four — Exercise

Research has proven that exercise helps to deal with anger. Whatever type you're comfortable with, I want you to do. If it's cycling, jogging, stretching, aerobic, boxing and don't forget our very own dancing. Yes, dancing. It's my best way to exercise, and it helps me feel good, just syncing with the music and allowing it to cleanse my heart. Jogging is also great because I embrace the fresh air and see people around. Please do your research and whatever is good for you, do it.

Tips for Day Four

- Don't procrastinate exercising. Just as it helps you stay fit, it also boosts your mood and helps to soothe your angry mind.

- You can exercise daily, but if it's not convenient for you, list out the days you'd be chanced and enjoy yourself.

- I understand if you say you can't exercise in your moment of anger, but have you tried a mental exercise while in a clear state of mind? It helps a whole lot.

Day Five — Get a Stress Ball

I found out there's a medical explanation for carrying a stress ball around from my research.

Scientists say that the limbic part of the brain is where our emotions are, and stress balls stimulate nerves in the hand that connects to these limbic parts. In simpler terms, when you press a stress ball in anger, it helps you feel better, especially for small amounts of fury, high-stress levels, and anxiety. It worked a lot for one of my friends and what was even more astounding was the fact that she could carry a stress ball anywhere.

Tips for Day Five

• I think you should add a stress ball to your shopping list and give it a try.

• Stress balls help us cope with anger. It teaches us discipline because we're careful not to lash out at anyone but pour out wrath by pressing the stress ball.

• The stress ball is a great friend for people coping with anger; it doesn't complain but understands and supports you in this fight. I do too.

Day Six: Find People To Vent To.

Dear black woman, have you heard of anger support groups? It's a great way to check on your anger because you can identify with people who are going through similar anger issues with you. You meet and talk about your anger and its causes and solutions. I did this personally when the stress ball didn't seem to help me.

Tips for Day Six

• Stress balls may not work for you if your level of anger is at a high rate, so you might need to find other ways.

• Talking about your anger helps way more than you know it. It's a whole lot better way than keeping it in and letting it swallow you up.

• During my anger support group, I realized my anger issues were nothing compared to some people's own.

Day Seven - Go Over Everything

I require only one thing from you on this day, my black queen; that you go over everything we've done since day one. Did you breathe in during your fit of anger? Did it help you see the bright side of things? Have you forgiven and let go? How's your exercise coming? I hope you found the perfect one for you? Did you get that stress ball or opt for the support group? Don't tell me you did none; it would be unfair to me and my hard work writing this plan. Or did you do everything? Kudos, my beautiful black woman! Kudos! How's it been so far?

Tips For Day Seven

- Reflection is one of the significant tools for assessing oneself

- After consideration, even if you did not do everything thoroughly and ideally, don't be so hard and disappointed in yourself. Go again, and harder!

Week Two: Drain That Jealousy Out Of Your System

Day Eight - Acknowledge The Impact Of Jealousy

Many ladies fail to understand that it's natural to get jealous, but it doesn't mean it's a good thing. However, rather than accept that they're jealous and seek possible solutions out of its firm grip, they choose to deny the fact, thereby prolonging its effects. Accept you're jealous and accept the impact you've felt from jealousy.

Tips for Day Eight

- Many people are dying inside because they'd rather not admit to being jealous.
- The first step to getting rid of that jealousy is accepting that you are jealous.
- Are you with your pen? Can you write out a list of the effects of that jealousy? Can you see it's not helping you?

Day Nine- Find The Root

Once you finish accepting your jealousy and its impact, you have to begin clipping its grip out from your body, and the next step is to find the root cause of your jealousy. What's its trigger? Is it your friend's promotion? Your younger brother's marriage? Is your partner away on a business trip with another female? Whatever it is, you've got to figure it out.

Tips For Day Nine

- Once you finish accepting your jealousy, you have to find the cause.
- Take the whole day to look around you and make your observations.
- At your convenient time, whip out your pen and write down the cause of your jealousy. Look over it for a while and take a deep breath.

Day Ten - Let Your Voice Out

You can go through this step by talking to your partner or a third party. Let's say your partner is doing something to trigger jealousy in you rather than get angry at them; why don't you communicate. They might even be unaware. And if it's not something you can talk to a partner about, talking to a third party is always great. However, only do this with someone you trust.

Tips For Day Ten

•   Set out an appropriate and convenient time for you and your partner to communicate and let them know how you feel.
•   If the trigger for your jealousy isn't your partner and you can't talk about it with the person, you can always talk to any trusted friend.

Day Eleven: What Are Your Insecurities?

To master your emotions, you need to be truthful to yourself. Take your time to think about what your insecurities could be. Perhaps there are some underlying ones you might not know. This exercise is a step to knowing yourself better and would help deal with these insecurities you now know.

Tips For Day Eleven

• Please write down your insecurities and go over them.
• Some insecurities take a lot of self-confidence to go away.

• That insecurity could be the source of your jealousy.

Day Twelve - Begin Jealousy-Reducing Practices

These include practising gratitude for what you have. It also helps to reduce stress when you're grateful and content with your achievements. Realizing you're not where you were yesterday is a great spur to being thankful. Remind yourself of your self-worth and have it at the back of your mind that someone out there may be envious of your life, which should help boost your self-confidence. Lastly, practice coping techniques to help you at the moment. If you're overwhelmed with jealousy, you can try taking a walk, taking your time to do something calming, listening to music, writing your emotions down, and so on.

Tips For Day Twelve

• The activities for this day are quite a while lot. Split your time and begin each of them.

• I hope you're still with your notepad? List out ten amazing things about you.

• If you desire, get a notebook to write down your emotions.

Day Thirteen - Give it time

So far, you've come a long way in tackling jealousy. The practices you did the previous day are guaranteed to help you fight jealousy, and all you need is to give it time. So day thirteen, grab a cup of coffee, sip it in the most gentle and lady-like manner, and flip through the pages of your notepad. See how far you've come!

Tips For Day Thirteen

• Today doesn't require much from you other than relaxing and going through the previous tasks.

• Have fun today, and don't forget your daily exercise!

Day Fourteen: Talk to a therapist.

Here comes the final stage for mastering your jealousy, my dear black woman. If it's working positively for you, that's awesome, and I applaud your ability to master and bend it to your will. But if it still isn't despite all we've talked about, then it's a sign you have to see a therapist. Please don't be scared. It's not a bumpy ride.

Tips For Day Fourteen

• Everyone is different, and while what I've written for this second week might have helped you become better, for others, it hasn't.

• My next piece of advice is that you see a therapist who'll walk with you till you've overcome.

Week Three: Coping With Loneliness

Day Fifteen - Find a Hobby

Whatever may be the cause of your loneliness, probably a breakup, retirement, or loss of your loved one, it's understandable to grieve for weeks. But it would be best if you didn't let that loneliness lead to depression. Begin the fight against loneliness by doing the things you've always wanted to do. Stop procrastinating!

Tips For Day Fifteen
• Everyone has what they love to do. Find yours.
• If you've been using your busy schedule as an excuse not to do your hobby, you might as well start and get your mind occupied whenever you feel lonely.

Day Sixteen - Decide To Volunteer
Being a volunteer in a charity organization or any good organization not only fights loneliness but boosts your happiness. You get out of your house and meet new people while doing something good. It's a lovely feeling.

Tips For Day Sixteen
• It's a great idea to search for organizations around you to act as a volunteer.
• Doing service work to people can help get your mind off that thought for a while.

Day Seventeen - Rebuild Old Relationships

There have been some relationships you might have ignored for too long. My dear black woman, don't you think it's time you revive them? I'm talking about the ones that used to give you so much joy you never wanted to be anywhere if not with them. It's not too late to start rebuilding. If you're losing how to begin, I suggest you go through a mutual friend. Things would be a lot easier.

Tips For Day Seventeen

• Sometimes, we spend so much time on something or someone we forget the ones who used to bring us joy.

• In fighting loneliness, socializing is key, and what better way to start other than talking with old friends?

Day Eighteen: Get That Pet You've Always Wanted.

Getting a pet helps in many ways. First of all, they're great companions and true lovers, especially a dog which stays with you through thick and thin. Also, taking your dog out for a walk helps you meet new people and fellow dog-walkers. It also encourages you to exercise.

Tips For Day Eighteen

• Most people get a pet for companionship.

• When I was going through a heartbreak, I got myself a dog, and trust me; my dog helped keep me in the company that I shed tears the day she died.

Day Nineteen - Why Not Sports?

I ask this question again, why not sports? There are many benefits linked with engaging in sports; physical, emotional, social benefits. Engaging in team sports helps you meet new people and even make friends while fighting your loneliness.

Tips For Day Nineteen

• Participating in sports will serve as a health booster and help meet new people.

• You can also make friends and business partners through sports.

Day Twenty - Books And Socializing

Books and Socializing go together because of book clubs. Book lovers are usually interested in either being a part of a book club or setting up their own. People interested in books gather at a specific time to discuss books. It opens your mind to different people's thoughts and helps develop you mentally.

Tips For Day Twenty

• Book clubs are usually fun for book lovers.

• Take a walk out of your home and find a good book club around you.

Day Twenty-One - Find Online Support

Sometimes, you may be unable to associate with people, but trying online can be more accessible. If your loved ones are far away, chatting with them via social media platforms and video calling via Skype is a great way to combat loneliness. On the other hand, if you're looking for friendship online, it's great too, but you have to be extra careful to avoid scammers.

Tips For Day Twenty-One

• You can set up a social media account to connect with your loved ones far away.

• It would help if you trod with care while talking to strangers online; some are harbingers of evil.

Week Four: Stop Feeding That Guilt

Day Twenty-Two - Spell Out Your Guilt

Let's begin by stating your guilt. I hope you're with your notebook and pen. Whatever that's eating up your mind poorly, I need you to write down. This exercise is as easy as it can be and challenging because of the emotions that could overwhelm you, but I need you to be strong and do this. When you finish stating your guilt, think about what the source could be.

Tips For Day Twenty-Two

- Trying to suppress your guilt doesn't help matters. You have to admit and accept it.

- Guilt doesn't always have to be about what you've done. It can be a result of an experience, maybe surviving an accident.

- People can guilt-trip you when you're not wrong.

Day Twenty-Three - Say That Apology And Make Amends

Apologies always have to come before amendments. It requires you to apologize to whoever you've hurt and apologized to yourself. Oh yes, sometimes you deserve an apology when you cling to that guilt and blame yourself constantly. So if you've been beating yourself up as a form of punishment, I advise you to apologize to your beautiful self and make amends.

Tips For Day Twenty-Three

• Asking for forgiveness doesn't necessarily mean the person you've hurt would forgive you immediately or at all, but it helps you heal faster.

• Sometimes you need to tell yourself it isn't your fault and get over some things.

• To decide to make amends means you've decided to change, and that's a massive step to mastering your emotions.

Day Twenty-Four - Letting Your Guilt Teach You

How did day twenty-three go? Did you ask that person for forgiveness? What did they say? As I said earlier, some people may not forgive you because of how hurt they are, but you don't have to slide into depression, my black queen. Take solace in the fact that you're genuinely repentant and choose to move on. Work on that habit that marred your relationship; stop it if it's a bad one. Now you're going to need your notepad again. I need you to write out the lessons you've learned. What do you regret doing? What would you not want to do anymore?

Tips For Day Twenty-Four

•	Identify the behavior behind your guilt and work on it. It might take a while to find it, but once you do, be assured you've solved half of your problem.

•	Understand that you can't change your past, but you can work on the present.

Day Twenty-Five - Be Grateful For That Guilt

I know this is concise work, but let me share this story with you. We can't work every day and not have some fun, not so? A few weeks back, I was to go on a date with a lady, but I fell under the weather. Rather than be honest and go straight to the point, I told her I would make it, but I didn't, and to date, she sees me as a liar and untrustworthy person. It's funny if you look at it from an abstract perspective, but then again, it taught me never to lie. And up to date, I'm meticulous in telling the truth because I know the consequences can be grave at times. So be grateful for that guilt you're feeling; it helps you feel human. While being grateful, use it to your advantage rather than let it destroy you.

Tips For Day Twenty-Five

• Most negative emotions can be used to our advantage rather than breed more negative ones.

• Let your guilt guide you to become a better person.

Day Twenty-Six - Take It Easy On Yourself

I am hammering on what I said initially on day twenty-three. Forgive Yourself. It's your fault, I understand. But how long can you continue to wallow in depression and self-inflicted pain? If someone keeps guilt-tripping you, you've got to walk away from that person and take it easy on yourself. Allow yourself to heal, my dear black woman.

Tips For Day Twenty-Six

• Most people set stumbling blocks to their growth and happiness by refusing to forgive themselves

- It's okay to feel remorseful, but don't let that shame eat you up.

Day Twenty-Seven - Begin To Work On Your Self-Esteem

I understand that guilt and shame come hand in hand and feeling ashamed downthrows on your self-esteem. You're on a journey to becoming a much better you, and how can you do that without your self-esteem in place? Once you've forgiven yourself, begin to work on your self-esteem by declaring only positive words about yourself.

Tips For Day Twenty-Seven

- Learning to forgive yourself helps you overcome your shame

- If you want to boost your self-esteem, show compassion to yourself. Remember what we talked about self-love?

Day Twenty-Eight - Meet With Your Therapist

It's day twenty-eight already, my beautiful black woman. How far have you dealt with that guilt? Do you still feel so guilty? Then I may not understand how bad it is, so please talk to your therapist. Therapists know how best to handle things, and trust me, you'll feel better in no time.

Tips For Day Twenty-Eight

- An excellent step to showing yourself love is asking for help when you're unable to help yourself.

- There's no shame in telling someone you need help.

Week Five: Getting Over Disappointments

Day Twenty-Nine: Be Human; Feel.

When disappointed, please do not push it deep inside. It would only worsen matters because you'll still feel those emotions at unexpected times. It's not a death sentence to be disappointed. Maybe you hoped in someone or something or went the extra mile, and the results were the opposite of what you wished for, it happens sometimes, and that's okay. Trust me on this. So accept that disappointment, but DO NOT dwell in it for too long.

Tips For Day Twenty-Nine

• Don't hide your disappointment with a big smile, pretending everything is okay.

• Pretense kills faster than acceptance.

Day Thirty- Say To Yourself - You're Not A Disappointment

It's day thirty and the second day of this week. We just started on this journey, my beautiful black queen. I sincerely hope you're not tired. Now that you've accepted that disappointment and felt it, can you let me tell you that you're not a disappointment and you'd believe it? Do yourself the favor of going through the things you wrote about yourself and let yourself know that you're not a disappointment.

Tips For Day Thirty

• That you had a setback doesn't mean you're a failure.

• Because you were disappointed or disappointed in someone doesn't mean it can happen another time.
• If you step out of your comfort zone, disappointments are sure to occur at certain times.

Day Thirty-One - You're Not A god That Can Control Everything

As far as you cannot control everything in this life, my beautiful black woman has to be prepared for disappointments. People disappoint, and you are people, so sometimes it can happen to you. It's a natural phenomenon, so why exactly do you have to beat yourself up or it?

Tips For Day Thirty-One

• Setbacks are a sign that you're trying to grow, so it's alright.

• If you had no control over a situation, you should not feel guilty for what happened.

Day Thirty-Two - Constantly Seeking Perfection Can Be Unhealthy

If you're the type that always expects the actions of others to be perfect, sorry to burst your bubbles, but you're going to get disappointed more often than not. Do you remember what we discussed in Chapter Nine about perfection? So you should know the strains constantly seeking perfection may cause to you.

Tips For Day Thirty-Two

• It's only proper that you adjust your expectations from people and not expect too much.

• If you're a perfectionist, you might procrastinate a lot due to fear of your work not being perfect.

• Constantly expecting perfection from people can cause a strain on your relationship with them.

Day Thirty-Three: Learn from it.

When you stop wallowing in the sorrow that comes with disappointment, you'll be able to see your mistakes clearly and learn your lessons.

Tips For Day Thirty-Three

• Ask yourself what it is you can do differently next time.

• Also, think about the one thing you can learn from this experience.

Day Thirty-Four: Create Time For A Break.

Sometimes all you need is a break from everything. Instead of going back right in after a disappointment and overworking yourself, I suggest you take a break. Starting work again in a hazy state of mind is not advisable to create time from your busy schedule to recharge, and then you can begin.

Tips For Day Thirty-Four

• Don't rush your healing process. You're allowed to take your time.

• Another disappointment might crush you if you jump back in with no rest or plan.

Day Thirty-Five - Stop The Comparisons

My dear black woman, it's day thirty-five and the last day of this week. I hope you've understood that you're not supposed to wallow so much in your disappointments and that they're natural. A significant step to improving your self-esteem is to stop comparing yourself with others. Your achievements and their achievements are not the same because you're not the same person and everyone has a different time for their success story. Focus on yourself and start again with baby steps.

Tips For Day Thirty-Five

• There'll always be people ahead of you, but don't forget it's your race, and only yours.

• Rather than compare yourself with other people, why don't you compare yourself to your present self to your former self instead of comparing yourself with other people?

• Focusing on yourself is a helpful habit in building your self-esteem.

Week Six: Coping With Apathy

Day Thirty-Six - Identifying The Root Cause

It may be hard to find the cause of your apathy, especially when you don't take note of your emotions. Keeping a mental or physical record of your feelings can help you know why you're feeling indifferent. Be careful not to judge your feelings and try to understand yourself.

Tips For Day Thirty-Six

• Think back and check if any recent happening negatively impacted you.

• Check your daily routine if it's wearing you out, and change it.

Day Thirty-Seven - Begin That Old Hobby Again

Being in a numb state can be a whole lot as you slowly watch yourself losing a grip of all the things that once got you excited and gave you joy. My dear black woman, I need you to pause and think about what you loved doing and give them a try.

Tips For Day Thirty-Seven

• Was it singing that gave you joy? Try doing it again.

• Do you enjoy hanging out with friends? Or simply reading a book? Do whatever brings you joy.

Day Thirty-Eight - Open Your Mind To Only Positive Thoughts

Thoughts have the capacity of influencing how we feel, negative and positive thoughts alike. More often than not, negative reviews are bound to come in to unsettle you, but you have to stop them and declare positivity into your life.

Tips For Day Thirty-Eight

• Write out positive words in your notepad to declare over your life.

• Some positive words to say to yourself are, "I open my mind to positive ideas that will change my beliefs. I agree to change my life intentionally."

Day Thirty-Nine: Step Out Of Your Comfort Zone.

Endorphins are great mood boosters, and exercise helps in their release. So if you're feeling indifferent, it's best that you step out of your comfort zone and socialize with people and try activities. Anything but sit at home idling about.

Tips For Day Thirty-Nine

• You don't have to swim a thousand miles before you decide to exercise. Just taking a few steps for ten minutes will do great to boost your mood.

• The little steps can sometimes reverse even the most extreme apathy we take daily.

Day Forty - Meditate Daily

Meditation has been known since the onset to be a great mood booster. It helps you relax and experience ultimate tranquility, allowing your mind to be calm. Sometimes stress can be a factor of apathy, and all you need to do is meditate.

Tips For Day Forty

• Meditation helps to slow our minds and allow us to breathe correctly.

• You can always google ways to meditate if you're unsure where to start.

Day Forty-One - Celebrate Every Win

If your apathy results from your work, you're probably tired. I want you to look on the bright side and realize that you're still winning. Don't ignore the small wins, and make sure to take yourself on a date once in a while because you deserve to be spoilt.

Tips For Day Forty-One

• You can celebrate yourself by giving yourself gifts whenever you achieve something. It doesn't necessarily have to be significant.

• Have you worked all year long, and you're weary? Take a break and go on that vacation.

Day Forty-Two - Change Your Scenery

Your apathy could result from your environment, my beautiful black woman. As said in the tips for Day Forty-One, I think you deserve that vacation or even move out entirely. I know it sounds like running away when I talk about leaving your current environment altogether, but it isn't. See it as the motivation you may need to be interested in things again.

Tips For Day Forty-Two

• Even a weekend away from your place can do magic in boosting your mood.

• If your financial situation or work cannot allow that vacation, that's fine. You can still explore your neighborhood or even go hiking!

Week Seven: Putting Your Abusiveness In Check

Day Forty-Three – Admittance

First of all, I need you to get something straight. Abuse is not only about physical abuse. So while we walk together this week, I need you to have emotional, verbal, and physical abuse in mind. As a lady, physical abuse may not be as prevalent in you as in a man, but what about emotional and verbal abuse? You might see the signs of abuse in your relationship, but you might not find out in time that you're the abuser. The first step to getting rid of your abusive behavior is accepting that you're the problem and admitting it.

Tips For Day Forty-Three

•   When you pause to think about your actions, you might find out you're the one at fault.

•   That you're the abuser in your relationship doesn't mean you're a devil, but it isn't a good thing either, so you're going to have to work on it.

Day Forty-Four - Make A Commitment To Change

How did your reflection go yesterday? Did you find that you're at fault or not? If you are, I'm glad you've accepted. Today, we're going to do a little exercise. I want you to think about your actions to your partner, and if you want your relationship to get better, then you're going to have to commit to change. I understand that it's not going to be an easy process. Still, it's a habit you have to get rid of, so you can bookmark this page and look back at it every day for the rest of your journey and work towards it. You also have to change for your own sake and not just keep that relationship with your partner. This part is essential.

Tips For Day Forty-Four

- Sticking to old habits is a lot easier than changing, but you have to choose to be a better version of yourself.

- Have it in mind that change is never easy. Then think about the worthiness of this cause and make a decision.

Motivate yourself daily to work towards that change.

Day Forty-Five – Apologize

Many abusers don't deem it fit to listen to their partners and know how they feel. This step is crucial, and I suggest you do this carefully. Have a conversation with your partner and let them tell you how they think about some of your actions, and when you finish with that, do this - Apologize. No, don't explain yourself. Apologize.

Tips For Day Forty-Five
- Communication is crucial, but most people seem to ignore it. To know what you're doing to hurt your partner, you need to talk to them.

- Try to put yourself in their shoes and understand them. No one likes to suffer abuse, so you as the abuser should understand and ask for their forgiveness.

*   If you're no longer with that partner, you can still go ahead with this task to give you an idea of what to do and what not to do in your next relationship.

Day Forty-Six - Don't Give Excuses.

While you communicate with the person you're abusing or have abused, you might want to get defensive. I understand that abusive persons are not necessarily sadistic people but people in deep suffering. This deep suffering affects their self-esteem and makes them insecure and vulnerable, bringing others down in their sorry state. So if this is your case, giving excuses or justifying your actions will not help. Only let them understand what you're going through and ask for help or opt-out to go through it yourself without hurting anyone.

Tips For Day Forty-Six

*   People you abuse would not listen to your justification after you've abused them.

*   Let your partner know what you're going through and find ways to become a better you.

Day Forty-Seven - Forgive Yourself

I know it's a whole lot realizing that you're an abuser, but it's not a death sentence. It's what you've done, but it shouldn't define who you are. Everyone is capable of good within them. You can start forgiving yourself by taking responsibility for your actions rather than blaming others. This way, you can stop hurting other people and easily forgive yourself.

Tips For Day Forty-Seven

●   Everyone can change, and forgiveness is a significant step to change.

●   Abuse is something people do, but it isn't who they are. Don't let guilt eat you up poorly. Ask for forgiveness, forgive yourself and decide to change.

Day Forty-Eight - Don't Expect Too Much.

At times you can expect too much from your partner, probably because you're better than them in something or you're a perfectionist. You tend to get irritated when they don't match your expectations- thereby abusing them and blaming them for not meeting your expectations. You need to chill out and give them a break. No one is like you, so you shouldn't expect too much from anyone. Also, don't expect your partner to forgive you because you apologize. Some wounds may be too deep that they for you to ignore, but take solace in the fact that you've admitted to your flaws and chosen to be a better you.

Tips For Day Forty-Eight

●   Lowering your expectations of people sets you and them free from unnecessary patterns.

- Please don't blame your partner because he failed to meet your expectations.

- Focus on forgiving yourself without expecting forgiveness from others.

Day Forty-Nine - See A Therapist

Sometimes abuse doesn't always stem from the pain we feel but can include mental health conditions. I implore you, my beautiful black woman, to set aside a day to meet with a counselor or therapist and pour out your heart to them.

Tips For Day Forty-Nine

- Some people stop behaviors faster when they're seeing a therapist. You can give it a try if self-help isn't working for you.

- You may not know that you have a mental disorder causing your abuse; always seek professional help before things get out of hand.

Week Eight: Working On Your Passive-Aggressive Tendencies

Day Fifty - Recognizing Your Passive-Aggressive Behavior

To be passively aggressive means to show your anger in indirect ways like pouting, stubbornness, sulking, and so on. Have you thought about what your own is?

Tips For Day Fifty

- Observe yourself and know what your passive-aggressive behavior is.
- These behaviors don't develop in one day and will take time to change.

Day Fifty-One - Observe Other People

Another person may be exhibiting as much passive-aggressive behavior as you are showing in response to yours. Look out for them. Also, did you stop to wonder if you're overreacting?

Tips For Day Fifty-One

- Communication is more than talking and listening openly and directly. You also have to read the signs and unspoken messages.

Day Fifty-Two - Stop Being Sarcastic

Most passive-aggressive people resort to sarcasm in heated situations, but this only fuels fire.

Tips For Day Fifty-Two

• Some sarcastic words are, "yeah, right." "Whatever." "Good for you." Try to avoid them when in a quarrel.

Day Fifty-Three - Stop The Temporary Compliance

It happens when you accept a job and submit the task late, usually because of procrastination. If you feel unappreciated or underpaid, this could be a cause. Realize the effects of your behavior and work on the grounds of your temporary compliance.

Tips For Day Fifty-Three

• If you feel unappreciated, try to express your feelings rather than keep them.

• It's good to support your partner in doing the chores to quell passive aggression from building up in them.

Day Fifty-Four - Stop Intentionally Being Inefficient

If you're an employee, stop being hostile or stop giving less than required energy at work and then playing the victim card. You know how detrimental it can be to you and your organization, so you need to stop.

Tips For Day Fifty-Four

- If you're holding grudges with anyone, it's best to tell them.

- Inefficiency can manifest in taking a long time to wash the dishes because you're unhappy with doing the chore.

Day Fifty-Five - Face That Problem

Now it's time to stop your habit of passive aggression. Stop avoiding that problem and face it before it escalates into something big.

Tips For Day Fifty-Five

- Stop procrastinating or stalling at work or home because you don't want to face a problem.

- Avoiding problems and exhibiting passive aggression can cause people to become angry with you.

Day Fifty-Six - Avoid The Desire To Revenge Or Self-Deprecate

Stop spreading rumors about that person who upset you. Stop causing setbacks in that project because you're offended because you'd still be affected either way. Also, stop harming yourself because you're trying to get back at someone who might be unaware that they hurt you.

Tips For Day Fifty-Six

•	Sabotaging someone or something is an act of wickedness you should avoid.

•	Talk things through and let go of that judge.

Week Nine: Managing Stress and Anxiety

Day Fifty-Seven - Take A Break
If you're feeling stressed out, it's a sign that your body needs a break. Step back to relax.

Tips For Day Fifty-Seven

•	Listen to music, dance, do whatever helps relieve your stress.

Day Fifty-Eight - Get Enough Sleep

You might be anxious and stressed because you're not getting enough sleep.

Day Fifty-Nine - Eat Healthy

Do not skip meals and always eat balanced diets.

Tips For Day Fifty-Nine

•	Get a reminder to always eat on time.

- Do not stress-eat.

- Always carry healthy snacks around.

Day Sixty - Exercise Daily

Exercise as it boosts your self-esteem and reduces anxiety.

Tips For Day Sixty

- Taking deep breaths is a form of fitness.

- Count to ten slowly. You could exceed this number.

Day Sixty-One - Allow Yourself To Humour

Laughter, they say, is good medicine. So whenever you're stressed, listening to or watching comedies is an excellent way to relieve off your stress and anxiety.

Tips For Day Sixty-One

- Hanging out with friends can also bring you happiness.

- Allow yourself to find humor in most situations.

Day Sixty-Two - Know Your Triggers

Write out what's triggering your stress and anxiety in your notepad and look for ways to reduce these triggers.

Tips For Day Sixty-Two

- If work is stressing you, you should probably take a break.
- Going on a vacation away from that trigger is a great way to manage stress.

Day Sixty-Three - Talk To Someone

If you're still feeling anxious or stressed, you should probably see a therapist, counselor, or doctor.

Tips For Day Sixty-Three

- It's okay to tell your friends you're overwhelmed and need your private time.

Week Ten - Dealing With Embarrassments

Day Sixty-Four - It's In The Past

You need to understand that wallowing in the past will not help matters because you can't change your history. Embarrassments are bound to happen, and all you can do is move on.

Tips for Day Sixty-Four

- I know it can be hard to move on at times, but dwelling in your past won't help as well.

Day Sixty-Five - There's No Need To Apologize

It's a natural phenomenon to feel embarrassed, but you're not guilty of anything, so you don't have to apologize.

Tips for Day Sixty-Five

- You shouldn't apologize because you trip in front of people. These things happen.

Day Sixty-Six - Laugh It Out

As you know, embarrassment is in the past so do well to laugh at the incident as a means of letting go.

Tips for Day Sixty-Six

- It'll be easier to laugh at the situation when you can look at things from the proper perspective.

Day Sixty-Seven - Tell Someone Else

If you're not sure how to stop feeling embarrassed, you should tell your trusted friends about it. Who knows, they could even laugh about it with you, and you'd feel a whole lot better.

Tips for Day Sixty-Seven

- It's great to have a support system that makes you feel a whole lot better.

- Meeting with someone who wouldn't judge you and has gone through this experience is a blessing.

Day Sixty-Eight - It's Okay To Be Afraid

I understand that you're afraid to go to that place or try out that thing or see that person because of the embarrassment you faced. But you have to overcome that fear if you're going to be able to conquer it.

Tips for Day Sixty-Eight

•   Don't hinder your growth because of fear.

•   Believe that others also have things pricking their mind and that you're strong enough to overcome.

Day Sixty-Nine - Focus On The Present

Once you're able to deal with the embarrassments from your past, it's time, my beautiful black woman, to focus on the present.

Tips for Day Sixty-Nine

•   Focusing on the present helps you to stop dwelling in the past.

•   What do you intend to do now? Where are you now? Do you feel better? Ask these questions.

Day Seventy - Try Again

It's time to face your fears and try again. Have you avoided meeting that crush since the day you slipped in front of everyone, including him? You've got to stop hiding and try again.

Tips for Day Seventy

- Heal from that embarrassment and start being productive.

- Understand that sometimes, things can go wrong, and that's fine.

Week Eleven - Steps To Stop Feeling Self-Conscious

Day Seventy-One - Stop Thinking Negatively

An excellent step to stop feeling self-conscious is to accept that you think negatively and decide to stop it.

Tips for Day Seventy-One

If you're at the club and think someone is staring at you and mocking you inwardly, most times, it's not even true.

Day Seventy-Two - Stop Putting People On Pedestals

Stop believing everyone else is better than you because you have what it takes even to be better.

Tips for Day Seventy-Two

- We often feel insecure because we place others on pedestals who don't deserve such glorification.

- Remember that no one is perfect, and everyone has their bad moments.

Day Seventy-Three - Be Your Motivation

If your friend was in your situation, I'm guessing you would motivate them to feel better, so do the same for yourself.

Tips for Day Seventy-Three

- Think of what you'd tell your self-conscious friend to help them stop worrying.

- Read ego-boosting words to yourself.

- Have pep talks and show yourself excess love.

Day Seventy-Four - Love Yourself

Loving yourself entails accepting every part of you wholeheartedly, including that flaw. Know your strengths and work on them to boost your self-confidence.

Tips for Day Seventy-Four

- Focus on yourself and revel in your glory.

- Despite your flaws, remember that you have something to bring to the table that'll leave people wanting more.

Day Seventy-Five - You're Probably Overthinking Things

While you're worried about others, do you know that these people are jumbled up with thoughts?

Tips for Day Seventy-Five

• Most times, when we get out of the spotlight, we realize no one was looking, and it's all just in our heads.

• Did you stop to check if you're overthinking things?

Day Seventy-Six - Give It Your All

Rather than shrink back, it would be best to give your everything. If you're dancing before a crowd, go all in. That way, people will be excited to watch you, and they wouldn't even see through your Insecurities.

Tips for Day Seventy-Six

• Watching someone with enthusiasm helps them relax in their environment and allows zero room for anyone to judge them.

Day Seventy-Seven - Start From The Root Cause

Being self-conscious is unlikely to go away if you don't find the cause and deal with it quickly. Whatever is making you feel anxious, you have to face it bravely.

Tips for Day Seventy-Seven

- Remember our talk on courage? You'll need it to face the causes of your self-consciousness.

- Build your confidence by taking positive actions and celebrating those positive results.

Week Twelve- Handling Resentment

Day Seventy-Eight: Accept and feel your emotions. Don't ignore those feelings. Accept them.

Tips for Day Seventy-Eight

- Saying out loud what you feel helps you accept them

- Allowing those feelings to build inside of you will cause harm to you.

Day Seventy-Nine - What's Behind Your Resentment

Think about what made you feel this way. It could also be a person.

Tips for Day Seventy-Nine

- You can task yourself with remembering when these feelings started

- Your resentment could be because you feel unappreciated or overwhelmed.

Day Eighty - Stop Allowing Room For Those Negative Thoughts

It's normal to remember the past and feel terrible, but you have to stop those negative thoughts.

Tips for Day Eighty

• When you notice those negative thoughts will overwhelm you, distract yourself by doing an activity.

• Choosing to call a friend is a great distraction.

Day Eighty-one - Keep Track Of Your Feelings With A Journal

When you can not talk to someone about your emotions, venting out your resentment in your journal is another excellent option.

Tips for Day Eighty-one

• Writing allows you room to assess the situation from a different perspective and show you what is and what isn't.

Day Eighty-two - Talk To That Person

If you're having resentment against a person, it's best to talk to them about it.

Tips for Day Eighty-two

• Be assertive when you're stating what you do not like.
• If they refuse to change after you've talked to them, then you might have to let go.

Day Eighty-three - Don't Expect Too Much.

I think I've hammered on this enough that no one is perfect, so you shouldn't let yourself feel the disappointment of expecting too much.

Tips for Day Eighty-three

• If they fail to do something you wish they'd do, you can talk to them about it or take solace in the fact that they genuinely care.

• If at all they'll change, it'll take time, so be patient.

Day Eighty-four - See A Therapist

Harboring resentment can be detrimental to your health and cause depression to you. It can even affect your relationships with other people. Therefore, you should see a therapist or counselor to talk to them about your feelings.

Tips for Day Eighty-Four

• Therapists can help you through the stages of getting past resentment and provides techniques to help you cope.

Week Thirteen - Stopping The Habit Of Being Judgemental

Day Eighty-five - Know When You're Judging Someone

Be conscious of your thoughts and nip that judgmental thought in the bud by questioning the importance of those thoughts.

Tips for Day Eighty-Five

- If you think someone needs to lose weight, ask yourself how that's any of your business and opt for a compliment instead.
- If those thoughts do not benefit you, they shouldn't even be there in the first place.

Day Eighty-six - Take A Deep Breath

The frontal lobe of your brain helps you to be calm. Taking a deep breath activates it more.

Tips for Day Eighty-six

- Take deep breaths often so that it becomes a habit. It's helpful.

Day Eighty-seven - Be In Charge Of Your Thoughts And Feelings

Allowing disgust to control you makes you a slave to it. Be in charge of your emotions.

Tips for Day Eighty-Seven

- You're not entitled to feel disgusted. Don't convince yourself otherwise.

Day Eighty-Eight - Put Yourself In Their Shoes

You have to accept that you're not other people and that they have the right to their decisions. You have no control over them so try to understand their perspective instead of judging them.

Tips for Day Eighty-Eight

- It's unfair to judge someone without first hearing their story. Could you get to know them first?
- That person you're considering might be who he is because of his upbringing, but you're too blind to see it.

Day Eighty-Nine - Show Gratitude

As two fingers are not the same, you're not on the same level with certain persons. Express gratitude for where you are and to everyone who has helped you grow.

Tips for Day Eighty-Nine

- Remember to take a deep breath and wish them good whenever you feel tempted to judge someone or say something that would hurt them.

Day Ninety - Cultivate Compassion

My beautiful black woman, here we are. The last day! Go over everything we've talked about and cultivate the virtue of compassion in you. You won't judge anyone with it because you're moved to empathize with them.

Tips for Day Ninety

- A compassionate person is a happy person.

- To be human, you have to get rid of that negative thought about someone.

Conclusion

I had quite a lot of fun writing this book for you, my dear black woman. Every chapter was done to fill you with love, strength, motivation, and energy. They were also noted to spur you to action. To become a much better version of yourself who is full of potential and so much greatness.

I started this book with 'how to deal with negative emotions because I understood perfectly the turbulence of emotions. It is not an easy one to manage at all. I hope the tips in this book help you immensely. But, you have to be patient with yourself as well. The Italians would say poco a poco—little by little.

I explored self-love to understand what it means to love oneself truly. My dear, self-love is the most excellent romance ever. Love yourself wholly and proudly. It is the best thing you can do for yourself. I also explored courage. To do great things, even loving yourself, you would need a lot of courage. That is why I poured so much of myself into writing that chapter for you.

Did you enjoy the anxiety and self-worth chapters? I hope you did. Anxiety and self-worth issues are among the most significant problems black women usually face. I hope this book helps you deal with and manage them better. I also had great fun writing about beauty and body positivity. It is one

topic I love so much. I hope you never let the world
fill your head with so many ideas about beauty that
you forget the wonderful that you are. In one of the
chapters, beauty has no single definition. So, dare
to be beautiful as you are and define it your way.
I hope the mental health part of this book awakens
great zeal in you to care for your mental health
with all the tenderness in the world. It is essential.
Also, how did you enjoy the chapters about failures
and pedestals? My dear woman, I urge you not to
be afraid of failure. Live audaciously; it is okay to
fall. What matters the most is rising again. But,
never forget to learn lessons from every fall. Also,
love your life on your terms. Pedestals are limiting.
Don't walk through your life without the thrill you
desire.

The ninety-day plan will be of immense help to you
if you allow it to. Go through each day with love,
dedication, and intent. You would be amazed at
how well you would manage your emotions.

It is where we say goodbye, my dear black woman;
it was beautiful telling my stories to you in this
book and guiding you. Go on and be badass from
this moment on. I love you dearly.

Thank You

You could have picked from dozens of other books, but you picked our book **Emotional Self Care for Black Women.**

So, THANK YOU for getting this book and for making it all the way to the end.

Could you please consider posting a review on Amazon?

Posting a positive review is the best and easiest way to support the work of independent authors like me.

Your feedback will help me to keep writing the kind of books that will help you get the results you want.

It can be something short and simple ☺

Thank you so much